POCKET AMSTERDAM

updated by

BETH WILLIAMS

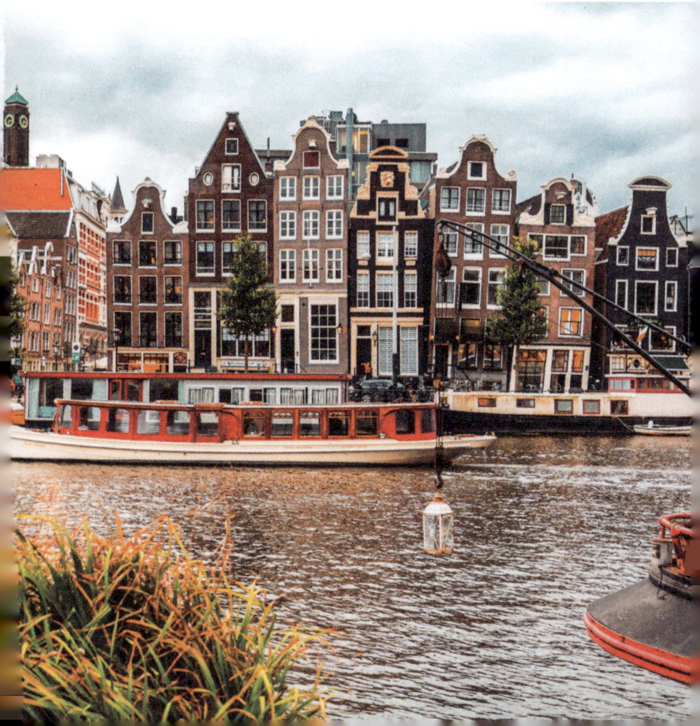

CONTENTS

AMSTERDAM

You could be sitting nursing a drink outside one of its cafés, chugging along its canals by boat, or riding its cheerful trams, and you'll know immediately that you couldn't be anywhere else in the world. What is it that makes the place so exceptional? Well, its watery cityscape means that much of the centre is off-limits to traffic; its architecture is iconic; and its people are a welcoming bunch. Amsterdam is always changing but has an uncanny ability to stay much the same as it has always been, no wonder it's one of the most popular tourist destinations in Europe.

Muziekgebouw aan 't IJ

In part it's the liberal traditions of the city that have given Amsterdam its distinctive character, beginning with the obvious legalized prostitution and dope-smoking coffeeshops. More subtle qualities are encapsulated by Amsterdammers themselves in the word *gezellig*, a very Dutch concept which roughly corresponds to "warmly convivial" – something perhaps most manifest in the city's wonderfully diverse selection of bars and cafés. Amsterdam is also riding something of a resurgent wave, with dozens of great new restaurants, a vibrant arts life and a club scene that has come of age. As if this wasn't enough, there's also the reinvention of neighbourhoods like De Pijp and the ambitious redevelopment of the old docklands bordering the River IJ, featuring glittering new public buildings such as the EYE film institute (see page 83) and the boho vibe of the former NDSM shipyard (see page 84).

Canalside drinking in the summer

All that said, the Old Centre remains the heart of the city, crowded and vital in equal measure. Spreading south from Centraal Station, and including Amsterdam's notorious Red Light District, the narrow canals of this district are bordered by old merchants' houses and a jangle of newer buildings reflecting Amsterdam's past and present glories. Moving on, the layout of the rest of the city centre is determined by a web of canals that loop right round the centre as the so-called Grachtengordel, a planned, seventeenth-century extension to the medieval town, with its tall, elegant gabled houses

When to visit

Amsterdam has warm, mild summers and moderately cold and wet winters. The climate is certainly not severe enough to make much difference to the city's routines, which makes Amsterdam an ideal all-year destination. That said, high summer – roughly late June to August – sees the city's parks packed to the gunnels and parts of the centre almost overwhelmed by tourists. Spring and autumn are not too crowded and can be especially beautiful, with mist hanging over the canals and low sunlight beaming through the cloud cover. Even in January and February, when the light can be at its gloomiest, there are compensations – wet cobbles glistening under the street lights and the canals rippled by falling raindrops. In the summer, from around June to August, mosquitoes can be bothersome.

What's New

A handful of new museums and galleries are set to open in 2025, including **Villa**, an immersive art gallery in Westerpark promising a hands-on experience with some of the best international and Dutch contemporary artists and the **DRIFT Museum**, another immersive space showcasing large-scale, tech-infused artworks in the expansive **Van Gendt Hallen**, a complex of five 19th-century. And yet, it is perhaps the old NDSM shipyard (page 84) that is most deserving of attention, its sprawl of old industrial buildings now accommodating all sorts of artistic endeavour – from art galleries through to boho bars and clubs.

reflected in olive-green waters. This is Amsterdam at its most beautiful, a perfect cityscape of balance and symmetry, its canals intercepted by a string of dinky humpback bridges. Just west of here is the Jordaan, a one-time working-class neighbourhood that has been much gentrified, and it's east to the Old Jewish Quarter with its memorials to the victims of the Holocaust.

Amsterdam also boasts a string of first-rate attractions, most notably the Anne Frank Huis, the Rijksmuseum, with its wonderful collection of Dutch paintings, the peerless Van Gogh Museum and the cleverly renovated Stedelijk gallery of modern and contemporary art. But it's not all about the sights: Amsterdam is a great city just to be in, with no attractions so important that they have to interrupt lazy days of wandering the canals and taking in the city at your own pace. Finally, don't forget that the Netherlands is a small country and there are plenty of compelling attractions close by, not least the small town of Haarlem, with the great Frans Hals Museum, the Zuider Zee villages to the north, and the stunning Keukenhof Gardens; even better, all very easy to reach by train and bus.

Brouwersgracht

Where to...

Shop

The **Nieuwendijk/Kalverstraat** strip in the Old Centre is home to high-street fashion and mainstream department stores, while nearby **Koningsplein** and **Leidsestraat** offer designer clothes, but the really up-market stuff is concentrated on **P.C. Hoofstraat**, near the Rijksmuseum. You'll find more offbeat clothes shops in the Jordaan and in the small radial streets that connect the main canals of the Grachtengordel – an area known as the Nine Streets. The cream of Amsterdam's antique trade is in the Spiegelkwartier, centred on **Nieuwe Spiegelstraat**.

OUR FAVOURITES: Droog see page 36. Boekie Woekie see page 53. Puccini Bomboni see page 54.

Eat

The **food** in the average Dutch restaurant has improved hugely in recent years, and there are many places serving inventive takes on homegrown cuisine with and without an emphasis on organic ingredients. The city also has a good assortment of ethnic restaurants, especially Indonesian, Surinamese, Chinese and Thai. There are lots of bars – known as *eetcafés* – that serve adventurous food for a decent price in a relaxed and unpretentious setting.

OUR FAVOURITES: Warung Spang Makandra see page 104. De Belhamel see page 56. Hemelse Modder see page 39.

Coffeeshops

Amsterdam is well-known for its **coffeeshops**, which are permitted to sell small quantities of **cannabis** and ready-made joints. The majority of coffeeshops are found in the Old Centre and generally look like regular cafés. Prevented from advertising (you need to look at a menu to see what's on offer) they usually sell a wide range of Dutch weed, grown under artificial lights, as well as compressed resin such as *Pollem*. Most of it is extremely potent and to be handled with care – ask before you buy to avoid any unpleasant surprises.

OUR FAVOURITES: La Tertulia see page 55. Happy Feelings see page 54. Katsu Coffeeshop see page 103.

Drink

Amsterdam's outstanding selection of bars range from traditional **brown cafés** – cosy places so called because of the dingy colour of their walls and general décor – to slick **designer bars**. The former often specialise in beers of every description, while the latter are as likely to focus on cocktails as they are on beer. Most places stay open until around midnight or 1am during the week, and until 2am at weekends. Look out for the few **tasting houses** or proeflokalen that have survived, originally the sampling rooms of small private distillers, now tiny, stand-up places specializing in jenever (gin). The clubbing scene is first-rate, and there are lots of bars with DJs, as well as an array of live music options, particularly for jazz.

OUR FAVOURITES: Het Papeneiland see page 58. In De Wildeman see page 41. De Drie Fleschjes see page 41.

Amsterdam at a glance

The Jordaan and western docklands page 60.

Amsterdam's old working-class heart, now firmly gentrified with a well-heeled air, but still retaining vestiges of its old roots. Don't miss the Pianola Museum.

The Old Centre page 24.

Most people's first encounter with Amsterdam is usually this lively district between Centraal Station and the Singel canal. Key attractions include the Koninklijk Paleis (Royal Palace), the Oude Kerk and Ons' Lieve Heer op Solder.

The Grachtengordel page 42.

The Amsterdam that everyone dreams of – peaceful canals, crisscrossed by humpbacked bridges and graced by elegant, gabled houses. Prime sights include Brouwersgracht, the Anne Frank Huis, De Gouden Bocht (Golden Bend), the Museum van Loon and the Museum Willet-Holthuysen.

The Museum Quarter and around page 88.

Home to the city's key museums – the Rijksmuseum, the Van Gogh Museum and the Stedelijk Museum - and the Vondelpark, the city's most enticing green space.

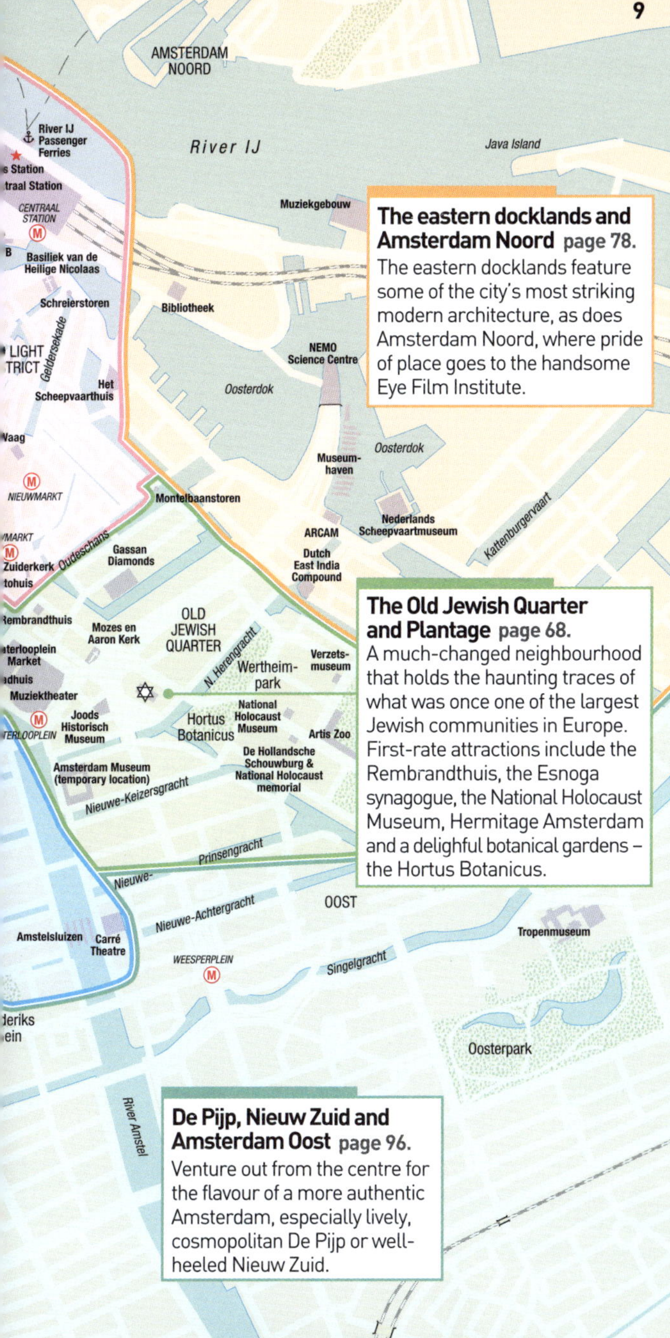

The eastern docklands and Amsterdam Noord page 78.

The eastern docklands feature some of the city's most striking modern architecture, as does Amsterdam Noord, where pride of place goes to the handsome Eye Film Institute.

The Old Jewish Quarter and Plantage page 68.

A much-changed neighbourhood that holds the haunting traces of what was once one of the largest Jewish communities in Europe. First-rate attractions include the Rembrandthuis, the Esnoga synagogue, the National Holocaust Museum, Hermitage Amsterdam and a delighful botanical gardens – the Hortus Botanicus.

De Pijp, Nieuw Zuid and Amsterdam Oost page 96.

Venture out from the centre for the flavour of a more authentic Amsterdam, especially lively, cosmopolitan De Pijp or well-heeled Nieuw Zuid.

15 Things not to miss

It isn't possible to see everything Amsterdam has to offer on a short trip, and we don't suggest you try. What follows is a selective taste of the city's highlights, in no particular order, from vibrant markets through to outstanding art collections. All entries have a page reference to take you straight into the Guide.

> Albert Cuypmarkt

See page 98

Busy and bustling general market that is still the authentic heart of working-class Amsterdam.

< Van Gogh Museum

See page 89

With the world's most comprehensive collection of the artist's work, this museum is simply unmissable.

∨ Rijksmuseum

See page 88

The city's biggest and best art museum with a wonderful collection of Golden Age (seventeenth-century) paintings.

< **Koninklijk Paleis**

See page 28

The supreme architectural example of the Dutch Golden Age, when the city was at the height of its powers.

∨ **Stedelijk Museum**

See page 91

Amsterdam's world-class modern and contemporary art museum is a prime attraction, its reach thoroughly international.

< **Anne Frank Huis**

See page 46

The secret annexe where the diarist hid with her family during the German occupation is Amsterdam's most moving tourist attraction.

∨ **Ons' Lieve Heer op Solder**

See page 30

Once a clandestine Catholic church, this seventeenth-century attic-chapel is an especially enjoyable sight.

∧ **Museum van Loon**
See page 50
This splendid mansion, sitting pretty beside the canal, boasts the city's finest seventeenth-century interior.

< **King's Day (April 27)**
See page 127
The one day of the year when anarchy reigns on the city's canals. Don't miss it.

∧ **Brouwersgracht**

See page 42

A string of handsomely renovated former warehouses make this one of the city's most picturesque canals.

∨ **EYE**

See page 83

The excellent EYE Film Institute occupies the city's finest new building, a sleek and graceful structure on the banks of the River IJ.

^ NDSM Shipyard

See page 84

Sprawling former shipyard now being renovated and refashioned with a New Age meets eco-boho vibe.

< Paradiso

See page 59

One of the city's oldest venues for live music, and still one of the best. In a capacious former church.

< The Nine Streets

See page 47

De Negen Straatjes hosts some of the city's quirkiest one-off stores – well worth a wander.

∨ Red Light District

See page 30

Right or wrong, Amsterdam's Red Light District is the real thing – and a big attraction in its own right.

Day One in Amsterdam

The Dam. See page 28. The heart of the city, and what better place to start than at this bustling and historic square?

Koninklijk Paleis. See page 28. The confidence and pride of the Golden Age – in a building.

Nieuwe Kerk. See page 29 No longer used as a church, but still one of the city's most impressive Gothic buildings.

Nine Streets. See page 47. These streets connecting the main canals are the epitome of what makes Amsterdam special – full of intriguing one-off designer shops, vintage boutiques, chic bars and cafés.

Lunch at Greenwoods. See page 55. Stop off for a club sandwich by the canal at this pocket-sized delight.

The Grachtengordel. See page 42. After shopping, just get lost in the web of stately seventeenth-century canals that make Amsterdam so unique.

Westerkerk. See page 46. Rembrandt's burial place, and the city's grandest Reformation-era landmark.

Anne Frank Huis. See page 46. The city's most renowned – and moving – sight, bar none.

The Jordaan. See page 60. One of Amsterdam's most wanderable and picturesque districts, full of independent stores, bars and restaurants.

Dinner at Moeders. See page 65. There's no better place to wind up of an evening than at this big, lively and very authentic Dutch restaurant on the edge of the Jordaan. Try the 'stampot' – a Dutch classic of mashed potatoes with vegetables and sausage.

Dam Square

Exploring the Grachtengordel

Restaurant in Jordaan

Day Two in Amsterdam

Rijksmuseum. See page 88. One of Europe's finest museums features an impressive array of works from some of the great Dutch masters: Rembrandt, Vermeer and Van Gogh.

Van Gogh Museum. See page 89. The greatest collection of the prolific nineteenth-century artist's work by far, and with good temporary exhibits that are worth a visit too.

Lunch at an Gent aan De Schinkel. See page 94. Stop for lunch at this great spot and savour the Belgian and fusion cuisine all on a lovely outside terrace as you watch the world go by.

Begijnhof. See page 35. Tucked away off the Spui, this is an alluring, unusual oasis of peace in the heart of the bustling city with a medieval church and immaculate fourteenth century homes.

Red Light District. See page 30. It's hard to come to Amsterdam and not have an evening wander around its most notorious neighbourhood.

Oude Kerk. See page 29. Despite being right at the centre of the notorius Red Light District, this is the city's most interesting and historic church.

Ons' Lieve Heer Op Solder. See page 30. This clandestine Catholic church, tucked away in an attic, is a real delight.

Dinner at Van Kerkwijk. See page 39. Great little bar/restaurant in the Old Centre. There's no menu – instead the friendly staff memorize the dishes of the day. However, one thing remains on the menu and that's the pear tart – make sure you leave ample space for it.

The Begijnhof

Red Light District

Dining in Van Kerkwijk

Jewish Amsterdam

Amsterdam's Jewish Quarter shows many reminders of how integral to the life of the city its Jewish population once was. Touring these sights makes for a moving day out.

Waterlooplein. See page 70. Home of the first Jewish settlement in Amsterdam, now the venue of the best flea market.

Joods Historisch Museum. See page 73. Four converted synagogues house permanent and temporary exhibits on Jewish life in the city.

Esnoga. See page 72. The city's imposing Portuguese Synagogue was once one of the largest in the world.

Hollandse Schouwburg – National Holocaust Memorial. See page 75. The remains of a theatre that was the main assembly point for Jews being deported in World War II.

Wertheimpark. See page 75. Tiny patch of greenery adorned by a moving memorial to those who died at Auschwitz.

Verzetsmuseum. See page 76. Excellent museum dedicated to the wartime resistance to the Germans.

Lunch at De Hortus. See page 77. Coffee, cake and snacks inside the city's botanical gardens.

Gassan Diamonds. See page 69. The only remnant of the main industry of the Jewish Quarter before the war.

Anne Frank Huis. See page 46. Not in the Jewish Quarter proper, but still the city's principal – and most essential – Jewish sight.

Dinner at Greetje. See page 86. Try out some tasty elevated Dutch cuisine at the snug *Greetje*.

Joods Historisch Museum

Hollandse Schouwburg

Gassan Diamonds

Cheap Amsterdam

It's possible to have a great day out in Amsterdam, see loads, and not spend a cent apart from a few euros on lunch and dinner. Here's how.

Begijnhof. See page 35. One of the city centre's most beguiling sights, and totally free.

Bloemenmarkt. See page 52. There's no charge to wander past the stalls of the city's wonderful flower market – but turn a blind eye to the tourist tat.

Lunch from a street vendor. Join the locals and order a cone of *frites* and mayonnaise from one of the many street vendors.

Albert Cuypmarkt. See page 98. Just wandering the length of the city's best market is a fine way to pass the time. Plus there's plenty of cheap street vendors here too.

Lunchtime concerts at the Concertgebouw/Muziektheater. See pages 92 and 69. There are regular free lunchtime concerts at these two impressive music venues.

Vondelpark. See page 93. The city centre's main park is one of its best attractions, and there's no charge for its weekend summer concerts either.

Zeeburg. See page 83. Take a walk or cycle around Amsterdam's up-and-coming districts to the east of Centraal Station.

Ferries across the IJ. See page 83. Take one of the free passenger ferries from behind Centraal Station to Amsterdam Noord and explore the emergent NDSM Shipyard and/or the EYE Film Institute.

Dinner at Warung Spang Makandra. See page 104. Fill up at this cheap, but delicious Surinamese-Javanese *eetcafé*. Don't miss the chicken satay. Also, a great spot for veggie and vegan dishes.

Eat like a local with frites and mayonnaise

Enjoying Vondelpark

The Zeeburg district

PLACES

Canal houses on the Prinsengracht

The Old Centre

Amsterdam's most vivacious district, the Old Centre is a tangle of antique streets and narrow canals, confined in the north by the River IJ and to the west and south by the Singel. Given the dominance of Centraal Station on most transport routes, this is where you'll almost certainly arrive. From here, a stroll across the bridge will take you onto the Damrak, which divided the Oude Zijde (Old Side) of the medieval city to the east from the smaller Nieuwe Zijde (New Side) to the west. It also leads to the heart of the Old Centre, Dam Square – usually known as the Dam – the site of the city's most imperious building, the Royal Palace (Koninklijk Paleis). Nowadays much of the Oude Zijde is taken up by the city's notorious Red Light District – but the area is about more than just sleaze: its main canals and the houses that line them are among Amsterdam's most handsome. And the Old Centre as a whole hosts some of the city's best bars and restaurants alongside what can only be described as tourist tat.

Centraal Station

MAP PAGE 26, POCKET MAP C10-11

Beurs van Berlage

At the time of its construction, on an artificial island in the 1880s, **Centraal Station** aroused much controversy because it effectively separated the centre from the River IJ, source of the city's wealth, for the first time in Amsterdam's long history. There was controversy about the choice of architect too: the man chosen, Petrus J.H. Cuypers, was Catholic, and in powerful Protestant circles there were mutterings about the vanity of his designs (he had recently completed the Rijksmuseum) and their unsuitability for Amsterdam. In the event, the station was built to Cuypers' design, but it was to be his last major commission; thereafter he spent most of his time building parish churches. The building has aged well and it's certainly a good place to arrive: its grand arches and cavernous main hall have a suitable sense of occasion, and from here all of the city lies before you.

Toil and trouble: the Noord-Zuidlijn

Ask the average Amsterdammer about the **Noord-Zuidlijn** and they may start frothing at the mouth: the plan to build a superfast, 10km-long metro line from the resurgent suburbs on the north side of the River IJ to a revamped transport hub on the south side of the city centre via Centraal Station may have seemed like a good idea when work began in 2003, but the execution was little short of a disaster. For a start, **tunnelling** beneath the city centre proved far more difficult than the contractors had envisaged, not least because many of the city's older buildings rest on wooden stilts which are easily disturbed – as indeed the opponents of the scheme had predicted in the first place. Time and again work was delayed while buildings were shored up or reinforced, and as a consequence **costs** spiralled – the original estimate of 1.46 billion guilders was soon eclipsed and when the line was finally completed in 2018 the overall cost had risen to over €3 billion, a staggering amount for a medium-sized city.

Basiliek van de Heilige Nicolaas

MAP PAGE 26, POCKET MAP D11
Prins Hendrikkade 73. nicolaas-parochie.nl. Free.

Dating back to the 1880s, the **Basiliek van de Heilige Nicolaas** is the city's foremost Catholic church, its whopping twin towers and cupola soaring over its immediate surroundings, though the spacious interior is distinctly gloomy. The church is dedicated to the patron saint of sailors – and of Amsterdam. Above the altar is the crown of the Habsburg Emperor Maximilian, perhaps surprisingly – given the breach with the Habsburgs in the seventeenth century – still very much a symbol of the city.

Damrak

MAP PAGE 26, POCKET MAP C11

Running from Centraal Station to Dam Square, **Damrak** was a canal and the city's main nautical artery until 1672, when it was filled in – much to the relief of the locals, who were tired of the stink. With the docks moved elsewhere, Damrak became a busy commercial drag, as it remains today: a crowded avenue lined with touristy restaurants, bars and bureaux de change.

Beurs van Berlage

MAP PAGE 26, POCKET MAP B11-C11
Damrak 243. beursvanberlage.com. Free, but charge for exhibitions & concerts.

The imposing bulk of the **Beurs** – the old Stock Exchange – is a seminal work designed at the turn of the twentieth century by the leading light of the Dutch modern movement, **Hendrik Petrus Berlage** (1856–1934). Berlage re-routed Dutch architecture with this building, forsaking the classicism that had dominated the nineteenth century for a modern style with cleaner lines. The Beurs has long since lost its commercial function and today it's used for exhibitions, concerts and conferences, which means that sometimes you can go in, sometimes you can't. Inside, the main hall is distinguished by the graceful lines of its exposed ironwork and its shallow-arched arcades as well as the fanciful frieze celebrating the stockbroker's trade. If it's closed, stop by the bistro that fronts onto Beursplein around the corner for a coffee and admire the tiled scenes of

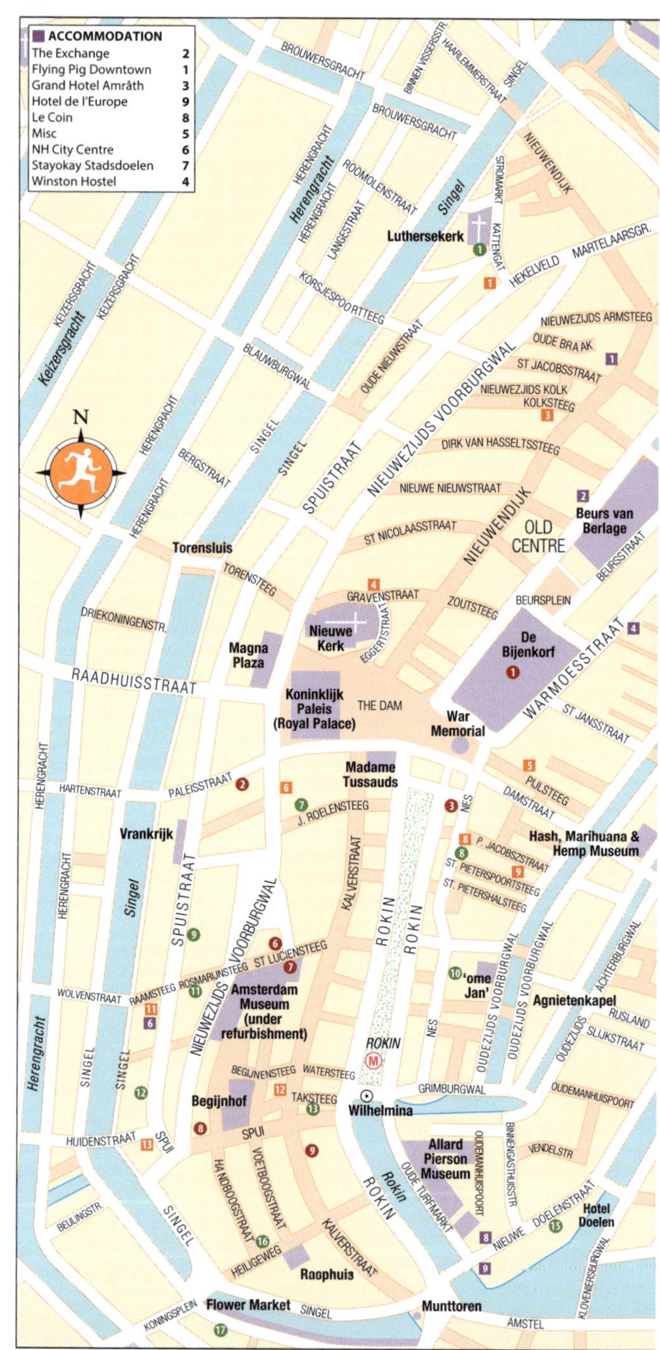
ACCOMMODATION
The Exchange 2
Flying Pig Downtown 1
Grand Hotel Amrâth 3
Hotel de l'Europe 9
Le Coin 8
Misc 5
NH City Centre 6
Stayokay Stadsdoelen 7
Winston Hostel 4
N
Luthersekerk
Torensluis
Magna Plaza
Nieuwe Kerk
Koninklijk Paleis (Royal Palace)
THE DAM
War Memorial
De Bijenkorf
Beurs van Berlage
OLD CENTRE
Madame Tussauds
Vrankrijk
Hash, Marihuana & Hemp Museum
Amsterdam Museum (under refurbishment)
'ome Jan'
Agnietenkapel
Begijnhof
Wilhelmina
Allard Pierson Museum
Hotel Doelen
Raophuis
Flower Market
Munttoren
ROKIN
BROUWERSGRACHT
HAARLEMMERSTRAAT
BINNEN VISSERSSTR.
SINGEL
NIEUWENDIJK
STROMARKT
KATTENGAT
HEKELVELD
MARTELAARSGR.
Herengracht
HERENGRACHT
ROOMOLENSTRAAT
LANGESTRAAT
Singel
KORSJESPOORTTEEG
Keizersgracht
KEIZERSGRACHT
BLAUWBURGWAL
OUDE NIEUWSTRAAT
NIEUWEZIJDS VOORBURGWAL
NIEUWEZIJDS ARMSTEEG
OUDE BRAAK
ST JACOBSSTRAAT
NIEUWEZIJDS KOLK
KOLKSTEEG
DIRK VAN HASSELTSSTEEG
BERGSTRAAT
SPUISTRAAT
NIEUWE NIEUWSTRAAT
ST NICOLAASSTRAAT
BEURSSTRAAT
TORENSTEEG
GRAVENSTRAAT
ZOUTSTEEG
BEURSPLEIN
DRIEKONINGENSTR.
EGGERTSTRAAT
WARMOESSTRAAT
RAADHUISSTRAAT
ST JANSSTRAAT
HARTENSTRAAT
PALEISSTRAAT
J. ROELENSTEEG
NES
PIJLSTEEG
DAMSTRAAT
P. JACOBSZSTRAAT
ST. PIETERSPOORTSTEEG
ST. PIETERSHALSTEEG
KALVERSTRAAT
NIEUWEZIJDS VOORBURGWAL
ST LUCIENSTEEG
ROSMARIJNSTEEG
RAAMSTEEG
WOLVENSTRAAT
OUDEZIJDS VOORBURGWAL
OUDEZIJDS ACHTERBURGWAL
RUSLAND
SLIJKSTRAAT
BEGIJNENSTEEG
WATERSTEEG
GRIMBURGWAL
OUDEMANHUISPOORT
TAKSTEEG
HUIDENSTRAAT
SPUI
HANDBOOGSTRAAT
VOETBOOGSTRAAT
Rokin
OUDE TURFMARKT
BINNENGASTHUISSTR
VENDELSTR
DOELENSTRAAT
NIEUWE
BEULINGSTR.
HEILIGEWEG
KLOVENIERSBURGWAL
KONINGSPLEIN
AMSTEL

The Old Centre
SHOPS
Akkerman 9
American Book Center 8
De Bierkoning 2
De Bijenkorf 1
Droog 10
Jacob Hooij 4
Laundry Industry 6
The Oh Collective 5
Posthumus 7
Puccini Bomboni 11
Scheltema 3
COFFEESHOPS
Abraxas 7
Dampkring 16
Kadinsky 11
CAFÉS & TEAROOMS
De Bakkerswinkel 3
Espressobar Puccini 14
Gartine 13
De Jaren 15
RESTAURANTS
Bird Thais 4
De Compagnon 2
Hemelse Modder 6
Lucius 9
Mappa 10
Nam Kee 5
Sampurna 17
De Silveren Spiegel 1
Van Kerkwijk 8
d'Vijff Vlieghen 12
BARS
De Bekeerde Suster 7
Bubbles & Wines 8
De Buurvrouw 9
Café de Dokter 12
De Drie Fleschjes 4
De Engelbewaarder 10
Gollem 11
Hoppe 13
In de Wildeman 3
In 't Aepjen 2
Wynand Fockink 5
CLUBS & VENUES
Bitterzoet 1
Club NL 6
River IJ Passenger Ferries
Bus Station
River IJ
Centraal Station
CENTRAAL STATION
Tourist Office
GVB
PRINS HENDRIK-KADE
Basiliek van de Heilige Nicolaas
DAMRAK
Damrak
NIEUWE BRUGSTEEG
ZEEDIJK
Schreierstoren
OUDE ARMSTEEG
BRUGSTEEG
H. HOEKSSTEEG
LANGE NIEZEL
Ons' Lieve Heer op Solder
KORTE NIEZEL
GELDERSKADE
Geldersekade
KROME WAAL
Het Scheepvaarthuis
Oude Kerk
RED LIGHT DISTRICT
OUDEZIJDS VOORBURGWAL
STORMSTEEG
WAALSTEEG
BINNEN BANTAMMERSTRAAT
ZEEDIJK
MOLENSTEEG
NIEUWE JONKERSTRAAT
NIEUWE LASTAGEWEG
NIEUWE RIDDERSTRAAT
RECHT BOOMSSLOOT
OUDEZIJDS ACHTERBURGWAL
MONNIKENSTRAAT
BLOEDSTRAAT
Waag
NIEUWMARKT
KONINGSTRAAT
BARNDESTEEG
Montelbaanstoren
KOESTRAAT
KEIZERSSTRAAT
BETHANIENSTRAAT
Kleine Trippenhuis
ST ANTONIESBREESTRAAT
DIJKSTRAAT
KORTE KONINGSTRAAT
KROMBOOMSSLOOT
OUDESCHANS
Oudeschans
OUDE HOOGSTRAAT
Trippenhuis
KLOVENIERSBURGWAL
NIEUWE HOOGSTRAAT
Zuiderkerk
Pintohuis
RAAMGRACHT
ZWANENBURGWAL
Gassan Diamonds
JODENBREESTRAAT
GROENBURGWAL
VERVERSSTRAAT
Rembrandthuis
Mozes en Aaron Kerk
WATERLOOPLEIN
STAALSTRAAT
Waterlooplein Market
Stadhuis
Muziektheater
AMSTEL
TURFSTEEG
Joods Historisch Museum
Esnoga
Dokwerker
0 metres 100
0 yards 100

The beautiful Basiliek Heilige Nicolaas

the past, present and the future by the Dutch artist Jan Toorop (1858–1928).

The Dam

MAP PAGE 26, POCKET MAP B12

At the very heart of the city, **Dam Square** – usually known as **The Dam** – gave Amsterdam its name: in the thirteenth century the River Amstel was dammed here, and the fishing village that grew around it became known as "Amstelredam". Boats could sail into the Dam down the Damrak and unload right in the middle of the settlement, which soon prospered by trading herrings for Baltic grain. Today it's an open and airy but somehow rather desultory square, despite the presence of the main municipal war memorial, a prominent stone tusk adorned by bleak, suffering figures and decorated with the coats of arms of each of the Netherlands' provinces (plus the ex-colony of Indonesia).

Madame Tussauds

MAP PAGE 26, POCKET MAP B12

Dam 20, Ⓦ madametussauds.com/amsterdam. Charge.

The Amsterdam branch of the **Madame Tussauds** empire provides waxwork Dutch royals and footballers alongside the usual international celebs. Very pricey.

Koninklijk Paleis

MAP PAGE 26, POCKET MAP B12

The Dam. Ⓦ paleisamsterdam.nl. Charge.

Dominating The Dam is the **Koninklijk Paleis** (Royal Palace), though the title is deceptive, given that this vast structure started out as the city's town hall and only had its first royal occupant in 1808 when Louis Bonaparte, brother of Napoleon, moved in during the short-lived French occupation.

At the time of the building's construction in the mid-seventeenth century, Amsterdam was at the height of its powers, and the city council craved a residence that was a suitable declaration of its wealth and independence. The **exterior** is full of maritime symbolism, hinting at the trade routes that made the city rich. The **interior** proclaims the pride and confidence of Amsterdam's Golden Age, principally in the lavish **Citizen's Hall** where the enthroned figure of Amsterdam looks down on the earth and the heavens, laid out before her in three circular, inlaid marble maps. Other allegorical **figures** ram home the municipal point: flanking "Amsterdam" to the left and right are Wisdom and Strength, and the relief to the right shows Mercury attempting to lull Argos to sleep – stressing the need to be vigilant. All this is part of a witty symbolism that pervades the Hall and the surrounding galleries: in the top-left gallery, cocks fight above the entrance to the Commissioner of Petty Affairs and above the door of the Bankruptcy Chamber, in the gallery to the right of the main hall, a medallion shows the Fall of Icarus below marble carvings depicting hungry rats nibbling at unpaid bills.

The decorative whimsy fizzles out in the intimidating and cramped **High Court of Justice** at the front of the building. Here, magistrates sat on marble benches overseen by heavyweight representations of Righteousness, Wisdom and Mercy as they passed judgement on the hapless criminals in front of them; even worse, the baying crowd on The Dam could view the proceedings through the barred windows. If a death sentence was passed, the condemned was whisked up to a wooden scaffold attached to the front of the building and promptly dispatched.

Nieuwe Kerk

MAP PAGE 26, POCKET MAP B12
The Dam. Ⓦ nieuwekerk.nl. Admission charge varies.

Vying for importance with the Royal Palace is the adjacent **Nieuwe Kerk**, which despite its name – "new church" – is an early fifteenth-century structure built in a late flourish of the Gothic style, with a forest of pinnacles and high, slender gables. Nowadays it's de-sanctified and used for temporary exhibitions. Opening times vary, and occasionally it's closed altogether when exhibitions are being changed, but it is worth going in if you can: its hangar-like interior holds a scattering of decorative highlights, such as the seventeenth-century tomb of Dutch naval hero Admiral Michiel de Ruyter, complete with trumpeting angels, conch-blowing Neptunes and cherubs all in a tizzy.

Magna Plaza

MAP PAGE 26, POCKET MAP A12
Nieuwezijds Voorburgwal 182.

Behind the Royal Palace, you can't miss the old neo-Gothic post office of 1899, now converted into the **Magna Plaza** shopping mall, housing numerous clothes chains and a food hall.

Oude Kerk

MAP PAGE 26, POCKET MAP C12
Oudekerksplein. Ⓦ oudekerk.nl. Charge.

Tucked away in the Red Light District, the **Oude Kerk** is the city's most appealing church. There's been a church on this site since the middle of the thirteenth century, but most of the present building dates from a century later, funded by the pilgrims who came here in their hundreds following a widely publicized miracle. The story goes that in 1345 a dying man regurgitated the Host he had received here at Communion and when it was thrown on the fire afterwards, it did not burn. The unburnable Host was placed in a chest and eventually installed here, and although it disappeared during the Reformation, thousands of the faithful still come to take part in the annual commemorative **Stille Omgang** in mid-March, a silent nocturnal procession terminating at the Oude Kerk.

Inside the church you can see the unadorned memorial tablet of Rembrandt's first wife, Saskia van Uylenburg, beneath (and just to the left of) the smaller of the organs, and four beautifully coloured **stained-glass windows** beside the ambulatory dating from the 1550s, though some of the contemporary art exhibitions that take place here pay little regard to these features.

Ons' Lieve Heer Op Solder

MAP PAGE 26, POCKET MAP C11
Oudezijds Voorburgwal 38.
Ⓦ opsolder.nl. Charge.

A few metres north of the Oude Kerk is the lovely **Ons' Lieve Heer op Solder** ("Our Dear Lord in the Attic"), a former Catholic chapel, now one of Amsterdam's most enjoyable museums. The church dates from the early seventeenth century when the city's ruling Protestants decreed that Catholics could no longer practise their faith openly. The result was an eccentric compromise: Catholics were allowed to hold services in any private building providing that the exterior revealed no sign of their activities – hence the development of the city's **clandestine churches** (*schuilkerken*), of which the Ons' Lieve Heer op Solder is the only one to have survived intact, here in the loft of a wealthy merchant's house. The church's narrow nave has been skilfully shoehorned into the available space and, flanked by elegant balconies, there's just enough room for an ornately carved organ at one end and a mock-marble high altar, decorated with Jacob de Wit's mawkish *Baptism of Christ*,

The Red Light District

The area to the east of Damrak, between Warmoesstraat, Nieuwmarkt and Damstraat, is the **Red Light District**, known locally as "De Walletjes" (Small Walls) on account of the series of low brick walls that contains its canals. The district stretches across the two narrow canals that once marked the eastern limits of medieval Amsterdam, **Oudezijds Voorburgwal** and **Oudezijds Achterburgwal**. The area is pretty seedy, although the legalized prostitution here has long been one of the city's most distinctive draws. It wasn't always so: the handsome facades of Oudezijds Voorburgwal in particular recall ritzier days when this was one of the wealthiest parts of the city, richly earning its nickname the "Velvet Canal".

There have been major changes made to the Red Light District in recent years. The political (and social) attitudes that had long allowed it to flourish started to change after Job Cohen became city mayor in 2001. As Cohen explained "We realised this [sex work in Amsterdam] was no longer about small-scale entrepreneurs, but that big-crime organisations are involved here in trafficking women, drugs...and other criminal activities". His instincts were confirmed in 2004 when an authoritative report concluded that the general set-up of 'window brothels' was, in fact, helpful to pimps and facilitated their control. Since then, the city council has considerably reduced the number of 'window brothels' and sex shops - and as a result the unpleasant undertow that once permeated the Red Light District has largely disappeared. What's more, the whole **future** of the Red Light District is under review with some politicians proposing that the Red Light District be closed altogether or moved way out of the city. At the moment, there's deadlock and it's hard to say quite how the issue will be resolved.

Amsterdam at night

at the other. The rest of the house is similarly untouched, its original furnishings reminiscent of interiors by Vermeer or De Hooch.

Hash, Marihuana & Hemp Museum

MAP PAGE 26, POCKET MAP C12
Oudezijds Achterburgwal 148.
Ⓦ hashmuseum.com. Charge.

The **Hash, Marihuana & Hemp Museum** claims to hold the "world's largest collection of cannabis-related artefacts" and features displays on different kinds of dope and the huge number of ways to imbibe and otherwise use it. Among the six thousand items on show are old tins of prescription cannabis, a hemp electric guitar and running shoes, plus pamphlets explaining the medicinal properties of weed. There's also a shop selling pipes, books, videos and plenty of souvenirs.

Nieuwmarkt

MAP PAGE 26, POCKET MAP C12

On the far side of the Red Light District is the Nieuwmarkt, a wide open cobbled square that was long one of the city's most important markets. Its focus is the multi-turreted **Waag**, a delightful building dating from the 1480s, when it served as one of the city's fortified gates, the Sint Antoniespoort. Thereafter it was turned into a municipal weighing-house (*waag*), with the rooms upstairs taken over by the surgeons' guild. It was here that the surgeons held lectures on anatomy and public dissections, the inspiration for Rembrandt's famous *Anatomy Lesson of Dr Tulp*. It has now been converted into a café-bar and restaurant, *In de Waag*.

Schreierstoren

MAP PAGE 26, POCKET MAP D11-12
Geldersekade.

A few minutes' walk north from Nieuwmarkt, the squat **Schreierstoren** (Weepers' Tower) is a rare surviving chunk of the city's medieval wall. Originally, the tower overlooked the River IJ and it was here (legend has it) that women gathered to watch their menfolk sail away – hence its name. A badly weathered stone plaque inserted in the wall is a reminder of all those sad goodbyes, and another much more recent plaque recalls the departure of Henry Hudson from here in 1609, when he stumbled across an island the locals called Manhattan.

Het Scheepvaarthuis

MAP PAGE 26, POCKET MAP D11-12
Prins Hendrikkade 108.
Now occupied by the five-star *Amrath* hotel, this is one of the city's most flamboyant Expressionist buildings, covered with a welter of maritime references – the entrance is shaped like the prow of a ship, and surmounted by statues of Poseidon and his wife and representations of the four points of the compass.

Kloveniersburgwal

MAP PAGE 26, POCKET MAP C12-13
Nieuwmarkt lies at the northern end of **Kloveniersburgwal**, a long, dead-straight waterway framed by old, dignified facades. One house of special note is the **Trippenhuis**, at no. 29, a huge overblown mansion built for the Trip family in 1662. One of the richest families in Amsterdam, the Trips were one of a clique of families (Six, Trip, Hooft and Pauw) who shared power during the city's Golden Age.

Almost directly opposite the Trippenhuis, on the west bank of the canal, the **Kleine Trippenhuis** at no. 26 is, by contrast, one of the narrowest houses in Amsterdam, complete with a warmly carved facade with a balustrade featuring centaurs and sphinxes. Legend asserts that Mr Trip's coachman was so taken aback by the size of the new family mansion that he exclaimed he would be happy with a home no wider than the Trips' front door – which is exactly what he got.

St Antoniesbreestraat

MAP PAGE 26, POCKET MAP C12-13
Stretching southeast from the wide-open spaces of the Nieuwmarkt, **St Antoniesbreestraat** once linked the city centre with the Jewish quarter, but its huddle of shops and houses was mostly demolished in the 1980s to make way for a main road. The plan was subsequently abandoned, but the modern buildings that now line most of the street hardly fire the soul, even if the modern symmetries – and cubist, coloured panels – of the apartment blocks do lighten the aesthetic gloom.

Pintohuis

MAP PAGE 26, POCKET MAP D13
St Antoniesbreestraat 69 ⓣ 020 370 0210, ⓦ huisdepinto.nl. Free.
One of the few survivors of all the development along St Antoniebreestraat is the **Pintohuis**, which is now a cultural centre. Easily spotted by its creamy Italianate facade, the mansion is named after Isaac de Pinto, a Jew who fled Portugal to escape the Inquisition and subsequently became a founder of the East India Company. Pinto bought the property in 1651 and promptly had it remodelled in grand style, the facade interrupted by six lofty pilasters, which lead the eye up to the blind balustrade. The mansion was the talk of the town, even more so when Pinto had the interior painted in a similar style to the front – pop in to look at the birds and cherubs of the original painted ceiling.

Zuiderkerk

MAP PAGE 26, POCKET MAP C13
Zuiderkerkhof ⓦ zuiderkerkamsterdam.nl. Open for special events and concerts only.
The **Zuiderkerk** dates from 1611 and was designed by the prolific architect and sculptor Hendrick de Keyser, whose distinctive – and very popular – style extrapolated elements of traditional Flemish design, with fanciful detail added wherever possible. The soaring tower is typical of his work and comes complete with balconies and balustrades, arches and columns. The church was deconsecrated in the 1930s, and it was here that the

bodies of the dead were temporarily stored and piled up during the terrible winter – the "Hunger Winter" – of 1944–45.

Oudemanhuispoort

MAP PAGE 26, POCKET MAP B13-C13

At the south end of Kloveniersburgwal, on the right, the **Oudemanhuispoort** is a covered passageway whose sides are lined with secondhand bookstalls (Mon–Fri noon–5pm); it was formerly part of an almshouse complex for elderly men – hence the unusual name. The buildings to either side of the passageway are now part of the University of Amsterdam, which dominates this part of town, its associated colleges and residences stretching south to Nieuwe Dolenstraat.

Staalstraat

MAP PAGE 26, POCKET MAP C14

A dinky little bridge spans the southern end of Kloveniersburgwal to reach pedestrianized **Staalstraat**, which cuts across one of the most picturesque corners of the city on its way to Waterlooplein (see page 70). Staalstraat offers an especially lovely view down **Groenburgwal**, a narrow and almost impossibly pretty waterway framed by dignified old canal houses with the Zuiderkerk (see page 70) looming beyond.

Rokin and Kalverstraat

MAP PAGE 26, POCKET MAP B12-14

The **Rokin** picks up where the Damrak (see page 70) leaves off, cutting south from the Dam in a wide sweep that follows the former course of the River Amstel. This was the business centre of the nineteenth-century city, and although it has lost much of its prestige, it is still flanked by an attractive medley of architectural styles incorporating everything from grandiose nineteenth-century mansions to more utilitarian modern stuff. Running parallel, pedestrianized **Kalverstraat** is a busy shopping street that has been a commercial centre since medieval times, when it was used as a calf market; nowadays it's mostly chain stores and clothes shops – you could be anywhere in Europe really.

Reading in Pintohuis

Allard Pierson Museum

MAP PAGE 26, POCKET MAP B13-14
Oude Turfmarkt 127. Ⓦ allardpierson.nl. Charge.

The **Allard Pierson Museum** is a good old-fashioned archeological museum spread over two floors. It's not an especially large collection, but it does have a wide-ranging assortment of artefacts mainly retrieved from Egypt, Greece and Italy. The ground floor is used for both temporary exhibitions and the Egyptian pieces, among which is a fascinating section on the **Coptic Christians**, who still account for around ten percent (eight million) of the Egyptian population. Also of note is a delightful model of a ship and its crew from the Middle Kingdom – a funerary object designed to transport the soul of the dead to the afterlife. Upstairs, the highlight is the museum's Greek **pottery**, with superb examples of both the black- and red-figured wares produced in the sixth and fifth centuries BC. Look out also for several ornate Roman **sarcophagi** – especially the whopper made of marble and decorated with Dionysian scenes – as well as Etruscan funerary urns and carvings.

Heiligeweg and Spui

MAP PAGE 26, POCKET MAP A14

Heiligeweg, or "Holy Way", which crosses Kalverstraat near Muntplein, was once part of a much longer route used by pilgrims heading into Amsterdam. All religious references disappeared centuries ago, but there is one interesting edifice here, the fanciful gateway of the old **Rasphuis** (House of Correction) at the junction of Heiligeweg and Voetboogstraat. The gateway is surmounted by a sculpture of a woman holding the shield of authority punishing two criminals chained at her sides above the single word "Castigatio" (punishment). Beneath is a carving by Hendrik de Keyser showing wolves and lions cringing before the whip.

Cut up Voetboogstraat and you soon reach the **Spui**, which opens out into a wide, tram-clanking intersection. Right in the middle is a cloying statue of a young boy, known as *'t Lieverdje* ("Little Darling" or "Loveable Scamp"), a gift to the city from a cigarette company in

The Begijnhof

1960. It was here in the mid-1960s, with the statue seen as a symbol of the addicted consumer, that those playful political mavericks, the anarchic **Provos**, organized some of their most successful public pranks. There's a small secondhand book market here on Friday mornings.

Begijnhof

MAP PAGE 26, POCKET MAP A13
Spui. ⓦ begijnhofkapelamsterdam.nl. Free.

A little gateway on the north side of the Spui leads into the **Begijnhof**, where a huddle of immaculately maintained old houses looks onto a central green; if this door is locked, try the main entrance, 200m north of the Spui on Gedempte Begijnensloot. The Begijnhof was founded in the fourteenth century as a home for the *beguines* – members of a Catholic sisterhood living as nuns, but without vows and with the right of return to the secular world. The original medieval complex comprised a series of humble brick cottages, but these were mostly replaced by the larger, grander houses of today shortly after the Reformation, though the secretive, enclosed design survived.

The **Engelse Kerk**, beside the central green, is of medieval construction, but it was taken from the *beguines* and given to Amsterdam's English community during the Reformation. It's of interest for the carefully worked panels on the pulpit, which were designed by a youthful Piet Mondriaan. The *beguines*, meanwhile, celebrated Mass inconspicuously in the clandestine Catholic **Begijnhof Kapel**, which they established in the house opposite their old church, and this is still used today, a homely and very devout place, full of paintings and with large balconies on either side of the main nave.

Amsterdam Museum

MAP PAGE 26, POCKET MAP A13
Sint Luciënsteeg 27 & Kalverstraat 92. ⓦ amsterdammA13useum.nl. Closed for refurbishment until at least 2025. In the meantime, parts of the collection are displayed at Amstelhof on the Amstel River (see page 74). Charge.

Currently in the throes of a major refurbishment (due to be completed in 2025), the **Amsterdam Museum** occupies the rambling seventeenth-century buildings of the former municipal orphanage, including an open-air **courtyard**, where a set of wooden lockers show where the orphans would stow their kit, and a **glassed-in passageway** – the **Schuttersgalerij** – which has long been used for temporary exhibitions of group portraits – anything from Johan Cruyff and his footballing chums to paintings of the Amsterdam militia in their seventeenth-century pomp. When it reopens, the main part of the museum will survey the city's development from its origins as an insignificant fishing village to its present incarnation as a major metropolis. The permanent collection holds a scattering of paintings from the city's Golden Age plus a wide miscellany of items from the 1940s onwards. Quite how these will be organised when the museum reopens is impossible to predict, but hopefully certain features will be retained – like the displays on the demise of the Amsterdam shipbuilding industry, the squatters' movement and the Provos youth movement. Curiously, the museum also possesses – and hopefully this will also reappear – a so-called "White Car" (*De Witkar*), which looks something like a golf buggy and was part of an early environmental move to do something about the city's traffic congestion: the idea was that these simple, publicly-owned vehicles would be the only ones allowed in the city centre. By 1979, there were 35 on the road, but the more reactionary climate of the 1980s put paid to the whole idea.

Shops

Akkerman

MAP PAGE 26, POCKET MAP B13
Langebrugsteeg 13. ⓦ pwakkerman.com.
This is far and away the city's poshest pen shop, with an excellent selection of pens and writing accessories –from fountain pens to ball points, rollerballs and pencils.

American Book Center

MAP PAGE 26, POCKET MAP A13
Spui 12. ⓦ abc.nl.
This place has a great stock of books in English, from novels through to guidebooks, and is one of the city's best sources of English-language magazines and newspapers.

De Bierkoning

MAP PAGE 26, POCKET MAP A12
Paleisstraat 125. ⓦ bierkoning.nl.
The "Beer King" is aptly named: 950 different beers and counting, all with the appropriate glasses to drink them from – just in case you thought beer-drinking could be taken lightly.

De Bijenkorf

MAP PAGE 26, POCKET MAP B12
Dam 1. ⓦ debijenkorf.nl.
One of the city's best department stores, De Bijenkorf (literally 'beehive') is good for clothes, accessories and more especially kids' stuff - there's an excellent toy department.

Droog

MAP PAGE 26, POCKET MAP C14
Staalstraat 7b. ⓦ droog.com.
Founded in 1993, Droog has made a serious contribution to contemporary design. Some of their products, such as their milk-bottle chandelier, have ended up in museum collections; this is their gallery, café and shop, a shrine to both simplicity and artiness with attention-grabbing furniture, clothes and household objects.

Jacob Hooij

MAP PAGE 26, POCKET MAP C12
Kloveniersburgwal 12. ⓦ jacob-hooy.nl.
In business at this address since 1778, this is a traditional homeopathic chemist with any amount of herbs and natural cosmetics, as well as a huge stock of *drop* (Dutch liquorice).

Laundry Industry

MAP PAGE 26, POCKET MAP B13
Sint Luciensteeg 18.
ⓦ laundryindustry.com.
Just off Kalverstraat, this is the main Amsterdam branch of the cool, high-end Dutch women's and men's wear brand: great clothes, usually youthful, and a nice environment for browsing.

The Oh Collective

MAP PAGE 26, POCKET MAP C13
Oude Hoogstraat 12.
ⓦ theohcollective.com.
Welcoming, women-owned and LGBTQ+-friendly sexual wellness store offering a curated selection of sleek vibrators, libido-enhancing chocolates, organic cotton underwear, and plenty more to tickle your fancy.

Posthumus

MAP PAGE 26, POCKET MAP A13
Sint Luciensteeg 25. ⓣ 020 625 5812,
ⓦ posthumuswinkel.nl.
Top-of-the-range stationery, cards and, perhaps best of all, a choice of hundreds of rubber stamps. Ink pens – even quills – are another speciality here.

Puccini Bomboni

MAP PAGE 26, POCKET MAP C14
Staalstraat 17. ⓦ puccinibomboni.com.
The best chocolatier in town, selling an imaginative range of chocs in all sorts of shapes and sizes – try, for example, the fig marzipan chocolate or the cognac ganache consisting of cognac, raisins and cream. This mini-chain has also forsaken the tweeness of the traditional chocolatier for

brisk and bright modern decor. There's another outlet in the Grachtengordel (see page 54).

Scheltema

MAP PAGE 26, POCKET MAP B12
Rokin 9–15. Ⓦ scheltema.nl.
Amsterdam's biggest and probably best bookshop spreads over several floors. Although most of the books are in Dutch, there are good English sections too, one of the best being travel, which has a comprehensive selection of guidebooks, road maps and hiking maps. Special literary events are held here as well – check online or in-store for details.

Coffeeshops

Abraxas

MAP PAGE 26, POCKET MAP B12
Jonge Roelensteeg 12. Ⓦ abraxas.amsterdam.
Quirky, sometime psychedelic coffeeshop with spiral staircases that can be somewhat challenging later on in the evening. The hot chocolate with hash is not for the susceptible.

Dampkring

MAP PAGE 26, POCKET MAP A14
Handboogstraat 29. Ⓣ 020 638 0705.
Colourful coffeeshop with a laidback atmosphere that is known for its range of good-quality weed and hash. Used as a location in *Ocean's Twelve* starring Brad Pitt.

Kadinsky

MAP PAGE 26, POCKET MAP A13
Rosmarijnsteeg 9. Ⓦ kadinsky.nl.
The pick of a small chain of three coffeeshops; cosy and intimate with good deals, excellent chocolate chip cookies and a jazzy meets house soundtrack.

Abraxas

Puccini

Cafés and tearooms

De Bakkerswinkel

MAP PAGE 26, POCKET MAP C11
Warmoesstraat 69. ⓣ 020 489 8000, ⓦ bakkerswinkel.nl.
This is one of a popular chain offering delicious, home-made scones with lemon curd and jam, muffins, cakes, quiches and pies for just a few euros. Don't be surprised if you have to queue at lunchtime. €

Espressobar Puccini

MAP PAGE 26, POCKET MAP C14
Staalstraat 21. ⓦ puccini.nl.
Lovely little café that serves delicious breakfasts, salads and sandwiches from bright and cheerful premises. A few doors down from its sister chocolate shop (see page 54). A cake or a pastry here is a must. €

Gartine

MAP PAGE 26, POCKET MAP B13
Taksteeg 7. ⓦ gartine.nl.
Pocket-sized place down a narrow lane off one of the grungier stretches of Kalverstraat. Nice breakfasts, an array of inventive sandwiches for lunch, and then – their speciality – high tea served in the afternoon. Organic food too, often grown in their own kitchen garden. €

De Jaren

MAP PAGE 26, POCKET MAP B14
Nieuwe Doelenstraat 20. ⓦ cafedejaren.nl.
One of the grandest of the grand cafés, overlooking the Amstel next to the university, with three floors and two terraces. A great place to nurse the Sunday papers. Morphs into a restaurant and ultimately a bar in the evenings. The breakfasts here are a highlight with fresh pastries, smoothies and open sandwiches. €

Restaurants

Bird Thais

MAP PAGE 26, POCKET MAP D11

Zeedijk 72. thai-bird.nl.
This authentic Thai restaurant is nearly always packed, and rightly so. Lavish, Thai décor and an invitingly comprehensive menu. Incidentally, its little brother across the street serves much the same food in slightly more downbeat surroundings. €€

De Compagnon

MAP PAGE 26, POCKET MAP C11
Guldenhandsteeg 17. decompagnon.nl.
Tip-top French cuisine is on offer here at this smart and traditional restaurant. A typical main course is guinea fowl in a morels sauce. First-rate wine cellar too – and knowledgeable staff to help. Reservations advised. Three- to five-course set menus are the order of the day. €€€€

Hemelse Modder

MAP PAGE 26, POCKET MAP D12
Oude Waal 11. hemelsemodder.nl.
Welcoming Dutch restaurant serving extremely tasty meat and fish dishes in an informal, bistro-style atmosphere. One stand-out starter is their delicious shrimp with cognac foam and crayfish tail soup. The name "heavenly mud" refers to their dark and white chocolate dessert with vanilla cream. €€

Lucius

MAP PAGE 26, POCKET MAP A13
Spuistraat 247. lucius.nl.
This bistro-style restaurant, with its high-varnish wooden panelling, is one of the most popular fish restaurants in town. The lemon sole, when it's on the menu, is particularly excellent. Tends to attract an older clientele. Reservations advised. €€

Mappa

MAP PAGE 26, POCKET MAP B13
Nes 59. restaurantmappa.nl.
Classic Italian with inventive twists, incorporating good home-made pasta dishes and excellent service in an unpretentious, modern setting. They do a particularly good ravioli. Morphs into a bar when the kitchen closes at 10pm. €€

Nam Kee

MAP PAGE 26, POCKET MAP C12
Zeedijk 111–113. namkee.nl.
Arguably the best of a number of inexpensive Chinese diners along this stretch of the Zeedijk. Especially tasty starters – try the oysters in a black bean sauce. No frills modern décor in modest, unassuming premises. €

Sampurna

MAP PAGE 26, POCKET MAP A14
Singel 498. sampurna.com.
One of the city's favourite Asian restaurants, the *Sampurna* has been serving classic Indonesian cuisine in attractive, dimly lit surroundings for several decades. Offers the full range of Indonesian dishes with a competent wine cellar to wash it all down. €€€€

De Silveren Spiegel

MAP PAGE 26, POCKET MAP B10
Kattengat 4. desilverenspiegel.com.
This long-established really rather formal restaurant, "The Silver Mirror", is one of Amsterdam's finest, offering a delicately balanced menu of Franco-Dutch dishes, try, for example, the venison with artichokes and beetroot. Set menus at peak times, but otherwise à la carte. €€€€

Van Kerkwijk

MAP PAGE 26, POCKET MAP B12
Nes 41. vankerkwijk.com.
In brisk modern premises near the Dam, this welcoming restaurant serves steaks, fish and so forth, from an ever-changing unwritten menu that is heroically memorized by the attentive waiting staff. Good food – and a tasty sideline in salads. €

d'Vijff Vlieghen

MAP PAGE 26, POCKET MAP A13

Bubbles & Wines

Spuistraat 294. vijffvlieghen.nl.
One of the city's more formal restaurants, "The Five Flies" occupies immaculate premises kitted out in a smart version of antique Dutch style, from the tile- and wood-panelled walls to the beamed ceiling and antique embossed leather hangings. Intimate and atmospheric, its menu features imaginative renditions of traditional dishes, with herring and suckling pig being two favourites. €€€€

Bars

De Bekeerde Suster

MAP PAGE 26, POCKET MAP C12
Kloveniersburgwal 6. 020 423 0112, debekeerdesuster.nl.
A step up from the tawdry drinkeries of the neighbouring Red Light District, this popular bar – 'The Reformed Sister' – has a splendid long bar and incorporates its own micro-brewery – you might start off with the ever-so-tasty 'De Manke Monnik'.

Bubbles & Wines

MAP PAGE 26, POCKET MAP B12
Nes 37. 020 422 3318, bubblesandwines.com.
Over fifty wines by the glass in this appealing wine and champagne bar that attracts a well-heeled crew. In-the-know staff will help you decide. Smart and modern, salon-style décor.

De Buurvrouw

MAP PAGE 26, POCKET MAP B13
St Pieterspoortsteeg 29. debuurvrouw.nl.
Take a walk on the wild side at this dark, noisy bar where the music throbs way into the early hours. In the heart of the Red Light District – and it shows.

Café de Dokter

MAP PAGE 26, POCKET MAP A13
Roozenboomsteeg 4. 020 626 4427
Long-established brown café with stained glass and ancient

furnishings. Liqueurs fill the shelves behind the tiny bar, and the *ossenworst* (smoked sausage) is a meaty treat.

De Drie Fleschjes

MAP PAGE 26, POCKET MAP B12
Gravenstraat 18. Ⓦ dedriefleschjes.nl.
Cosy, antique and heartening tasting house for spirits and liqueurs – especially jenever, hence the long line of wooden barrels. Clients tend to be well heeled or well soused (or both).

De Engelbewaarder

MAP PAGE 26, POCKET MAP C13
Kloveniersburgwal 59. Ⓦ cafedeengelbewaarder.nl.
Once the meeting place of Amsterdam's bookish types, this is still known as a literary café. It's a relaxed and informal first-floor spot, with live jazz on Sunday afternoons (normally from 4.30pm). Canalside terrace too.

Gollem

MAP PAGE 26, POCKET MAP A13
Raamsteeg 4. Ⓦ cafegollem.nl.
Small and convivial, split-level brown bar with rickety furniture, wood panelling and a generous selection of Belgian beers, plus a few Dutch brews for variety – and with the correct glasses to drink them from.

Hoppe

MAP PAGE 26, POCKET MAP A13
Spui 18. Ⓦ cafehoppe.com.
One of Amsterdam's oldest and best-known bars, cramped and narrow with sawdust on the ancient wooden floor. Frequented by both the determined drinker and the city's businessfolk on their (very) wayward way home. Summer is especially good, when the throng spills (tumbles) out onto the street.

In de Wildeman

MAP PAGE 26, POCKET MAP B11
Kolksteeg 3. Ⓦ indewildeman.nl.
This lovely old-fashioned bar is housed in a former distillery and offers a huge range of beers (250 and counting) from around the world. A peaceful escape from the loud and tacky shops of nearby Nieuwendijk.

In 't Aepjen

MAP PAGE 26, POCKET MAP C11
Zeedijk 1. Ⓣ 020 428 8291.
A bar since the days when Zeedijk was the haunt of sailors on the razzle, and still one of the city centre's best watering holes. Get a plate of cheese or sausage to help the ale go down. The place gets its name – literally "In the Monkeys" – from the times when sailors ran out of guilders and bartered for extra drinks: some swapped their pet monkeys – hence the name.

Wynand Fockink

MAP PAGE 26, POCKET MAP B12
Pijlsteeg 31. Ⓦ wynand-fockink.nl.
Ancient and intimate bar tucked away down an alley off The Dam. It offers a vast range of its own flavoured jenevers, many of which they distil themselves in neighbouring premises.

Clubs and venues

Bitterzoet

MAP PAGE 26, POCKET MAP B11
Spuistraat 2. Ⓦ bitterzoet.com.
Spacious but surprisingly cosy two-floored bar and theatre hosting a mixed bag of events: DJ sets, live gigs featuring European indie bands, plus occasional poetry and film nights.

Club NL

MAP PAGE 26, POCKET MAP A12
Nieuwezijds Voorburgwal 169. Ⓦ clubnl.nl.
What used to be the city's first lounge bar turned into a stylish house club, frequented by designer-clad young and not-so-young things. A long, dark bar and a heaving dance floor.

The Grachtengordel

The Grachtengordel, or "girdle of canals", reaches right round the city centre and is without doubt the most charming part of Amsterdam, its lattice of olive-green waterways and dinky humpback bridges overlooked by street upon street of handsome seventeenth-century canal houses. It's a subtle cityscape, too – full of surprises, with a bizarre carving here, an unusual facade there, but it is the district's overall atmosphere that appeals rather than any specific sight, with the exception of the Anne Frank Huis. There's no obvious walking route around the Grachtengordel, and you may prefer to wander around as the mood takes you, but the description we've given below goes from north to south, taking in all the highlights on the way. On all three of the main canals – Herengracht, Keizersgracht and Prinsengracht – street numbers begin in the north and increase as you go south.

Brouwersgracht

MAP PAGE 44, POCKET MAP C1–D2

Running east to west along the northern edge of the three main canals is leafy, memorably picturesque **Brouwersgracht**. Originally, Brouwersgracht lay at the edge of Amsterdam's great harbour with easy access to the sea. This was where ships returning from the East unloaded their silks and spices and breweries flourished, capitalizing on their ready access to fresh water. Today, the harbour bustle has moved elsewhere, and the warehouses, with their distinctive spout-neck gables and shuttered windows, which were formerly used for the delivery and dispatch of goods by pulley from the canal below, have been converted into ritzy apartments. These have proved particularly attractive to actors and film producers. There are handsome merchants' houses here as well, plus moored houseboats and a string of quaint little swing bridges. Restaurants have sprung up too, including one of the city's best, *De Belhamel* (see page 56).

The pretty canals of Amsterdam

Noorderkerk

MAP PAGE 44, POCKET MAP C2

Noorderkermarkt. ⓦ noorderkerk.nl. Free.

Prolific architect Hendrik de Keyser's last creation, finished two

The canals

The **canals of the Grachtengordel** were dug in the seventeenth century in order to extend the boundaries of a city no longer able to accommodate its burgeoning population. Increasing the area of the city from two to seven square kilometres was a monumental task, and the conditions imposed by the council were strict. The **three main waterways** – Herengracht, Keizersgracht and Prinsengracht – were set aside for the residences and businesses of the richer and more influential Amsterdam merchants, while the radial cross-streets were reserved for more modest artisans' homes; meanwhile, immigrants, newly arrived to cash in on Amsterdam's booming economy, were assigned, albeit informally, the Jodenhoek (see page 68) and the Jordaan (see page 60). In the Grachtengordel, everyone, even the wealthiest merchant, had to comply with a set of detailed planning regulations. In particular, the council prescribed the size of each building plot – the frontage was set at thirty feet, the depth two hundred – and although there was a degree of tinkering, the end result was the loose conformity you can see today: tall, narrow residences, whose individualism is mainly restricted to the stylistic permutations amongst the **gables**.

The earliest gables, dating from the early seventeenth century, are the so-called **crow-stepped** gables, which were largely superseded by **neck gables** and **bell gables**, both named for the shape of the gable top. Some are embellished, some aren't, many have decorative cornices and the fanciest – which mostly date from the eighteenth century – sport full-scale balustrades. The plainest gables belong to the warehouses, where deep-arched and shuttered windows line up on either side of the loft doors that were originally (and often still are) used for loading and unloading goods winched by pulley from the street down below.

years after his death in 1623, this bulky brick building represented a radical departure from the conventional church designs of the time, having a symmetrical Greek-cross floor plan, with four arms radiating out from a steepled centre. Uncompromisingly dour, it proclaimed the serious intent of the Calvinists who worshipped here, its pulpit placed in the centre as a complete break with the Catholic past.

Noordermarkt

MAP PAGE 44, POCKET MAP C2

In the shadow of the Noorderkerk, the **Noordermarkt** is a substantial albeit rather unimpressive square, whose main item of interest is a statue of three figures bound to each other, representing a tribute to the bloody Jordaanoproer riot of 1934. The riot was part of a successful campaign to stop the government cutting unemployment benefits during the Depression; you'll find the statue just in front of the church's door. On Saturday's (9am–4pm) the square hosts one of Amsterdam's best **markets** – the farmers' market, **Boerenmarkt**.

Hofje Van Brienen

MAP PAGE 44, POCKET MAP C2
Prinsengracht 85–133. Free.

On the east side of Prinsengracht, opposite the Noorderkerk, this brown-brick courtyard was built as an almshouse (*hofje*) in 1804 by Aernout van Brienen. A well-to-do merchant, Van Brienen had locked

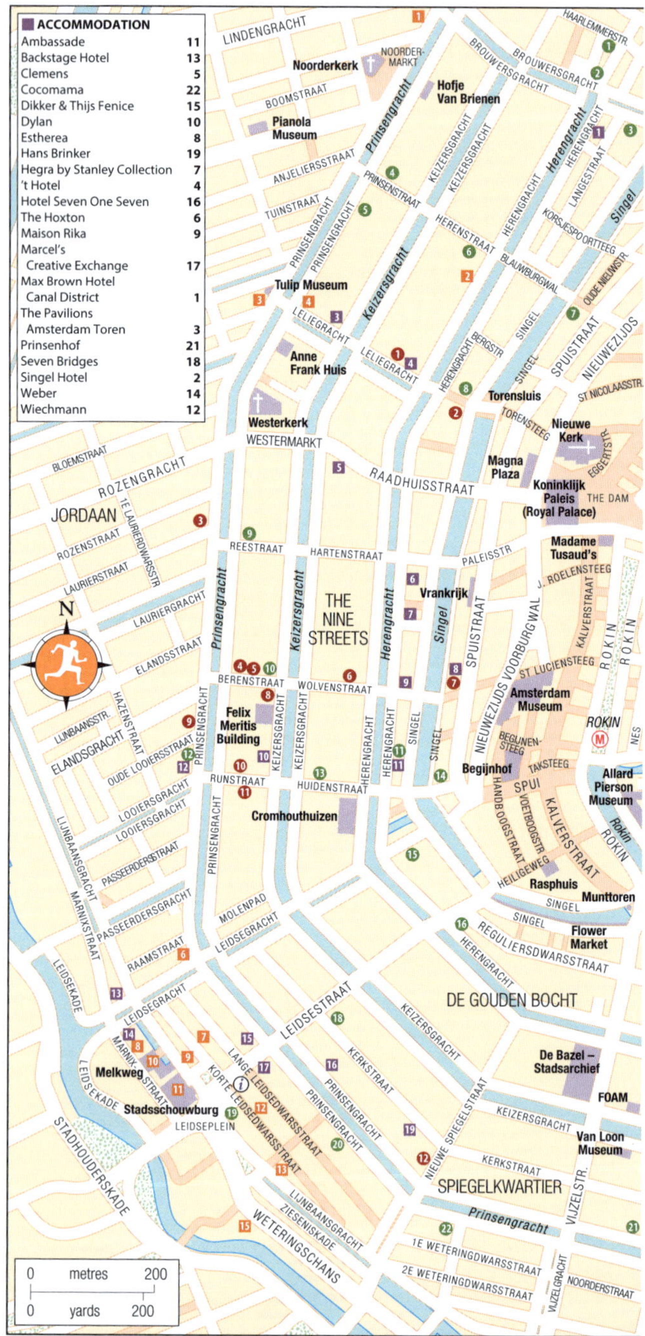

ACCOMMODATION
Ambassade 11
Backstage Hotel 13
Clemens 5
Cocomama 22
Dikker & Thijs Fenice 15
Dylan 10
Estherea 8
Hans Brinker 19
Hegra by Stanley Collection 7
't Hotel 4
Hotel Seven One Seven 16
The Hoxton 6
Maison Rika 9
Marcel's Creative Exchange 17
Max Brown Hotel Canal District 1
The Pavilions Amsterdam Toren 3
Prinsenhof 21
Seven Bridges 18
Singel Hotel 2
Weber 14
Wiechmann 12
Noorderkerk
Pianola Museum
Hofje Van Brienen
Tulip Museum
Anne Frank Huis
Westerkerk
Torensluis
Nieuwe Kerk
Magna Plaza
Koninklijk Paleis (Royal Palace)
THE DAM
Madame Tusaud's
JORDAAN
Vrankrijk
THE NINE STREETS
Felix Meritis Building
Amsterdam Museum
Begijnhof
Allard Pierson Museum
Cromhouthuizen
Rasphuis
Munttoren
Flower Market
DE GOUDEN BOCHT
De Bazel – Stadsarchief
FOAM
Van Loon Museum
Melkweg
Stadsschouwburg
LEIDSEPLEIN
SPIEGELKWARTIER
0 metres 200
0 yards 200

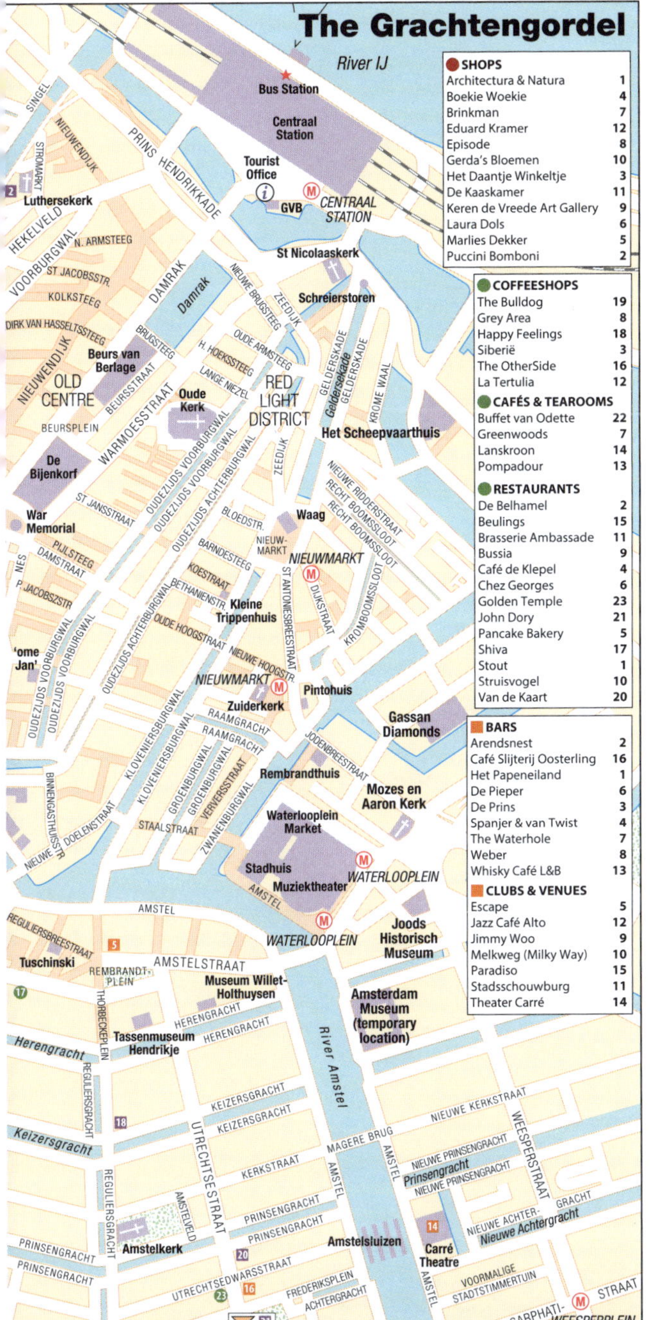
The Grachtengordel
SHOPS
Architectura & Natura 1
Boekie Woekie 4
Brinkman 7
Eduard Kramer 12
Episode 8
Gerda's Bloemen 10
Het Daantje Winkeltje 3
De Kaaskamer 11
Keren de Vreede Art Gallery 9
Laura Dols 6
Marlies Dekker 5
Puccini Bomboni 2
COFFEESHOPS
The Bulldog 19
Grey Area 8
Happy Feelings 18
Siberië 3
The OtherSide 16
La Tertulia 12
CAFÉS & TEAROOMS
Buffet van Odette 22
Greenwoods 7
Lanskroon 14
Pompadour 13
RESTAURANTS
De Belhamel 2
Beulings 15
Brasserie Ambassade 11
Bussia 9
Café de Klepel 4
Chez Georges 6
Golden Temple 23
John Dory 21
Pancake Bakery 5
Shiva 17
Stout 1
Struisvogel 10
Van de Kaart 20
BARS
Arendsnest 2
Café Slijterij Oosterling 16
Het Papeneiland 1
De Pieper 6
De Prins 3
Spanjer & van Twist 4
The Waterhole 7
Weber 8
Whisky Café L&B 13
CLUBS & VENUES
Escape 5
Jazz Café Alto 12
Jimmy Woo 9
Melkweg (Milky Way) 10
Paradiso 15
Stadsschouwburg 11
Theater Carré 14
River IJ
Bus Station
Centraal Station
Tourist Office
GVB
CENTRAAL STATION
St Nicolaaskerk
Schreierstoren
SINGEL
NIEUWENDIJK
STROMARKT
PRINS HENDRIKKADE
Lutherselkerk
HEKELVELD
N. ARMSTEEG
VOORBURGWAL
ST JACOBSSTR.
KOLKSTEEG
DAMRAK
Damrak
DIRK VAN HASSELTSSTEEG
BRUGSTEEG
NIEUWE BRUGSTEEG
ZEEDIJK
OUDE ARMSTEEG
H. HOEKSSTEEG
LANGE NIEZEL
NIEUWENDIJK
Beurs van Berlage
OLD CENTRE
BEURSSTRAAT
WARMOESSTRAAT
Oude Kerk
RED LIGHT DISTRICT
GELDERSKADE
Geldersekade
KROMME WAAL
Het Scheepvaarthuis
BEURSPLEIN
De Bijenkorf
OUDEZIJDS VOORBURGWAL
OUDEZIJDS ACHTERBURGWAL
ZEEDIJK
ST JANSSTRAAT
BLOEDSTR.
Waag
NIEUWE RIDDERSTRAAT
RECHT BOOMSSLOOT
War Memorial
NIEUW-MARKT
NIEUWMARKT
PIJLSTEEG
DAMSTRAAT
BARNDESTEEG
KOESTRAAT
BETHANIENSTR.
Kleine Trippenhuis
ST ANTONIESBREESTRAAT
DIJKSTRAAT
KROMBOOMSSLOOT
NES
P. JACOBSZSTR.
OUDE HOOGSTRAAT
NIEUWE HOOGSTR.
'ome Jan'
NIEUWMARKT
Pintohuis
Zuiderkerk
RAAMGRACHT
Gassan Diamonds
KLOVENIERSBURGWAL
GROENBURGWAL
JODENBREESTRAAT
Rembrandthuis
Mozes en Aaron Kerk
VERVERSSTRAAT
BINNENGASTHUISSTR.
DOELENSTRAAT
STAALSTRAAT
ZWANENBURGWAL
Waterlooplein Market
NIEUWE
Stadhuis
Muziektheater
WATERLOOPLEIN
AMSTEL
REGULIERSBREESTRAAT
WATERLOOPLEIN
Joods Historisch Museum
Tuschinski
REMBRANDTPLEIN
AMSTELSTRAAT
Museum Willet-Holthuysen
Amsterdam Museum (temporary location)
THORBECKEPLEIN
HERENGRACHT
Herengracht
Tassenmuseum Hendrikje
River Amstel
REGULIERSGRACHT
KEIZERSGRACHT
Keizersgracht
UTRECHTSESTRAAT
NIEUWE KERKSTRAAT
WEESPERSTRAAT
MAGERE BRUG
KERKSTRAAT
NIEUWE PRINSENGRACHT
Prinsengracht
AMSTELVELD
PRINSENGRACHT
NIEUWE ACHTERGRACHT
Nieuwe Achtergracht
Amstelkerk
Amstelsluizen
Carré Theatre
UTRECHTSEDWARSSTRAAT
FREDERIKSPLEIN
ACHTERGRACHT
VOORMALIGE STADSTIMMERTUIN
SARPHATISTRAAT
WEESPERPLEIN

Anne Frank Huis

himself in his own strongroom by accident and, in a panic, he vowed to build a *hofje* if he was rescued: he was and he did. The plaque inside the complex doesn't give much of the game away: it is simply inscribed with "For the relief and shelter of those in need."

Leliegracht

MAP PAGE 44, POCKET MAP C3

Leliegracht leads east off Prinsengracht, and is one of the tiny radial canals that cut across the Grachtengordel. It holds one of the city's finest Art Nouveau structures, a tall and striking building at the Leliegracht-Keizersgracht junction designed by Gerrit van Arkel in 1905. It was originally the headquarters of a life insurance company – hence the two mosaics with angels recommending policies to bemused earthlings.

Anne Frank Huis

MAP PAGE 44, POCKET MAP C3

Prinsengracht 263–267. Ⓦ annefrank.org. Charge. Entry by timed ticket only; purchase online.

Easily the city's most visited sight, the **Anne Frank Huis** is where the young diarist and her family hid from the Germans during World War II. Since the posthumous publication of her diaries, Anne Frank has become extraordinarily famous, in the first instance for recording the iniquities of the Holocaust, and latterly as a symbol of the fight against oppression and in particular racism. The family spent over two years in hiding here in a secret annexe between 1942 and 1944, but were eventually betrayed and dispatched to Westerbork – the transit camp in the north of the country where most Dutch Jews were processed before being moved to Belsen or Auschwitz. Of the eight souls hidden in the annexe, only Otto Frank survived; Anne and her sister died of typhus within a short time of each other in Belsen, just one week before the German surrender.

Anne Frank's **diary** was among the few things left behind in the annexe. It was retrieved by one of the people who had helped the Franks and handed to Anne's father on his return from Auschwitz; he later decided to publish it. Since its appearance in 1947, it has been constantly in print and has sold millions of copies.

Despite being so popular, the house has managed to preserve a sense of intimacy, a poignant witness to the personal nature of the Franks' sufferings. The rooms they occupied for two years have been left much the same as they were during the war, albeit without the furniture – down to the movie star pin-ups in Anne's bedroom and the marks on the wall recording the children's heights. Film clips of the family and the Holocaust give the background. Anne Frank was one of about one hundred thousand Dutch Jews who died during World War II, and her home provides one of the most enduring testaments to its horrors.

Westerkerk

MAP PAGE 44, POCKET MAP C3

Prinsengracht 281. Church ⓦ westerkerk.nl. Free. Tower ⓦ westertorenamsterdam.nl. Charge.

Trapped in her house, Anne Frank liked to listen to the bells of the neighbouring **Westerkerk**, until they were taken away to be melted down for the German war effort. The church still dominates the district, its 85m tower – without question Amsterdam's finest – soaring graciously above its surroundings. The church was designed by Hendrick de Keyser and completed in 1631 as part of the general enlargement of the city, but whereas the exterior is all studied elegance, the interior is bare and plain.

Westermarkt

MAP PAGE 44, POCKET MAP C3

Westermarkt, an open square in the shadow of the Westerkerk, possesses two evocative memorials. At the back of the church, beside Keizersgracht, are the three pink granite triangles (one each for the past, present and future) of the **Homomonument**, the world's first memorial to persecuted gays and lesbians, commemorating all those who died at the hands of the Germans. It was designed by Karin Daan and recalls the pink triangles the Nazis made homosexuals sew onto their clothes during World War II. Nearby, on the south side of the church by Prinsengracht, is a small but beautifully crafted **statue** of Anne Frank by the modern Dutch sculptor Mari Andriessen.

Westermarkt to Leidsegracht – The Nine streets

MAP PAGE 44, POCKET MAP C3-5

Between Westermarkt and Leidsegracht, the main canals are intercepted by a trio of cross-streets, which are themselves divided into shorter streets mostly named after animals whose pelts were once used in the district's tanning industry. There's Reestraat (Deer Street), Hartenstraat (Hart), Berenstraat (Bear) and Wolvenstraat (Wolf), not to mention Huidenstraat (Street of Hides) and Runstraat – a "run" being a bark used in tanning. The tanners are long gone and today these are eminently appealing shopping streets, known collectively as **De Negen Straatjes** (The Nine Streets).

Felix Meritis Building

MAP PAGE 44, POCKET MAP C4

Keizersgracht 324. ⓦ felixmeritis.nl.

A Neoclassical monolith of 1787, this mansion was built to house the artistic and scientific activities of the eponymous society, which was the cultural focus of the city's upper crust for nearly a hundred years. Dutch cultural aspirations did not, however, impress everyone. Legend has it that when Napoleon visited Amsterdam the entire building was redecorated for his reception, but he stalked out in disgust, claiming the place stank of tobacco. Oddly enough, it later became the headquarters of the Dutch Communist Party, but they sold it to the council who now lease it to the **Felix Meritis Foundation** for experimental and avant-garde art

Felix Meritis building

The Stadsschouwburg

workshops, conferences, discussions and debates.

Leidseplein

MAP PAGE 44, POCKET MAP C5

Lying on the edge of the Grachtengordel, **Leidseplein** is a bustling hub of city nightlife. The square once marked the end of the road in from Leiden and, as horse-drawn traffic was banned from the centre long ago, it was here that the Dutch left their horses and carts – a sort of equine car park. Today, it's quite the opposite: continual traffic made up of trams, bikes, cars and pedestrians gives the place a frenetic feel, and the surrounding side streets are jammed with bars, restaurants and clubs in a bright jumble of jutting signs and neon lights. On a good night, Leidseplein can be Amsterdam at its carefree, exuberant best.

Stadsschouwburg

MAP PAGE 44, POCKET MAP B5–C5

Leidseplein 26. ⓦ ita.nl.

Leidseplein holds the grandiose **Stadsschouwburg**, a clumpy neo-Renaissance edifice dating from 1894. At the time, it was so widely criticized for its clumsy vulgarity that the city council temporarily withheld the money for decorating the interior. Home to the National Ballet and Opera until the Muziektheater (see page 69) was completed on Waterlooplein in 1986, it is now used for theatre, dance and music performances, rebranded as the **International Theatre Amsterdam** (ITA). It also functions as the spot where the Ajax football team gather on the balcony to wave to the crowds whenever they win anything, as they often do.

Leidsestraat

MAP PAGE 44, POCKET MAP C5

Heading northeast from Leidseplein, **Leidsestraat** is a busy shopping street that leads across the three main canals up towards the Singel and the flower market.

Spiegelkwartier

MAP PAGE 44, POCKET MAP C6

One block east of Leidsestraat is **Nieuwe Spiegelstraat**, an appealing mixture of shops, stores and corner cafés that extends south into Spiegelgracht to form the

Spiegelkwartier – home to the pricey end of Amsterdam's antiques trade.

De Gouden Bocht

MAP PAGE 44, POCKET MAP D5

Nieuwe Spiegelstraat meets the elegant sweep of Herengracht near the west end of the so-called **De Gouden Bocht** (the **Golden Bend**), where the canal is overlooked by double-fronted mansions – some of the most opulent dwellings in the city. Most of these houses were remodelled in the late seventeenth and eighteenth centuries. Characteristically, they have double stairways leading to the entrance, underneath which the small door was for the servants, while up above, the majority of the houses are topped off by the ornamental cornices that were fashionable at the time. Classical references are common, both in form – pediments, columns and pilasters – and decoration, from scrolls and vases through to geometric patterns inspired by ancient Greece.

De Bazel – The Stadsarchief

MAP PAGE 44, POCKET MAP D6

Vijzelstraat 32. ⓦ debazelamsterdam.com. Free, but charge for exhibitions.

De Bazel, one of Amsterdam's weirdest and most incongruous buildings, stretches south down Vijzelstraat from Herengracht – you can't miss its looming, geometrical brickwork. Dating to the 1920s, this whopper of a structure was designed by the architect **Karel de Bazel** (1869–1923), whose devotion to theosophy formed and framed its design. Indeed, every facet of Bazel's building reflects the theosophical desire for order and balance, from the (faded) pink and yellow brickwork of the exterior (representing male and female respectively) to the repeated use of interior motifs drawn from the Middle East, the source of much

Han van Meegeren and the forged Vermeers

Keizersgracht 321, opposite the Felix Meritis building (see page 47), is in itself fairly innocuous, but these routine offices were once the home of the Dutch art forger **Han van Meegeren** (1889–1947). During the German occupation of World War II, Meegeren sold a "previously unknown" Vermeer to a German art dealer working for Herman Goering; what neither the dealer nor Goering realized was that Meegeren had painted it himself. A forger *par excellence*, Meegeren had developed a sophisticated ageing technique in the early 1930s. He mixed his paints with phenol formaldehyde resin dissolved in benzene and then baked the finished painting in an oven for several hours; the end result fooled everyone, including the curators of the Rijksmuseum, who had bought another "Vermeer" from him in 1941. The forgeries may well have never been discovered but for a strange sequence of events. In May 1945 a British captain by the name of Harry Anderson discovered Meegeren's "Vermeer" in Goering's art collection. Meegeren was promptly arrested as a collaborator and, to get himself out of a pickle, he soon confessed to this and other forgeries, arguing that he had duped the Nazis rather than helping them – though he had, of course, pocketed the money. It was a fine argument and his reward was a short prison sentence – but in the event he died from a heart attack before he could be locked up.

Museum Willet-Holthuysen

of the cult's spiritual inspiration. The building started out as the headquarters of a Dutch shipping company, the **Nederlandsche Handelsmaatschappij**, but is now home to a conference centre and the **Stadsarchief**, the vast city archives. A rotated selection of documents and photographs drawn from the archives is displayed in De Bazel's richly decorated Art Deco **Schatkamer** (Treasury).

Museum Van Loon

MAP PAGE 44, POCKET MAP D6
Keizersgracht 672.
museumvanloon.nl. Charge.

The **Museum Van Loon** boasts the finest accessible canal house interior in Amsterdam. Built in 1672, and first occupied by Ferdinand Bol, the artist and pupil of Rembrandt, the house has been returned to something akin to its eighteenth-century appearance, with acres of wood panelling and fancy stucco work. Look out also for the ornate copper balustrade on the staircase, into which is worked the name "Van Hagen-Trip" (after a previous owner of the house); the Van Loons later filled the spaces between the letters with iron curlicues to prevent their children falling through. The top-floor landing has several paintings sporting Roman figures, and one of the bedrooms is decorated with a Romantic painting of Italy, a favourite motif in Amsterdam from around 1750 to 1820. The oddest items are the fake bedroom doors: the eighteenth-century owners were so keen to avoid any lack of symmetry that they camouflaged the real bedroom doors and created imitation, decorative doors in the "correct" position instead. Out the back, beyond the little garden, stands the fancy **coach house**, which now holds an excellent display on exactly where much of the Van Loon fortune came from: the answer, the slave plantations of Suriname. The Dutch only abolished slavery in their colonies – and then rather reluctantly – in 1863. Slave owners were compensated to the tune of 300 guilders per slave.

FOAM

MAP PAGE 44, POCKET MAP D5
Keizersgracht 609. foam.org. Charge.

In a large and thoroughly refurbished old canal house, Amsterdam's leading photography museum **FOAM** (short for Fotografiemuseum) is achingly fashionable, its temporary exhibitions – of which there are usually four at any one time – featuring the best (or most obscure) of contemporary photographers. FOAM prides itself on its internationalism, though it does give space to famous or up-and-coming Dutch photographers like Carel Willink, Frido Troost and Otto Kaan. FOAM also offers guided, walk-through tours and photography workshops, both of which are extremely popular.

Museum Willet-Holthuysen

MAP PAGE 44, POCKET MAP E5

Herengracht 605. willetholthuysen.nl. Charge.

The coal-trading Holthuysen family occupied this elegant mansion until the last of the line, Louisa Willet-Holthuysen, gifted her home and its contents to the city in 1895. The most striking room is the **Men's Parlour**, which has been returned to its original nineteenth-century Rococo appearance – a flashy and ornate style that the Dutch merchants of the day regarded as the epitome of refinement and good taste. The house also displays a small but tasteful collection of fine and applied art assembled by Louisa's husband, Abraham Willet.

The Amstel and the Magere Brug

MAP PAGE 44, POCKET MAP E5-G9 & F6

The Grachtengordel comes to an abrupt halt at the River Amstel. The **Magere Brug** (Skinny Bridge), spanning the Amstel at the end of Kerkstraat, is the most famous and arguably the cutest of the city's many swing bridges. Legend has it that this bridge, which dates back to about 1670, replaced an even older and skinnier version, originally built by two sisters who lived on either side of the river and were fed up with having to walk so far to see each other.

Amstelsluizen

MAP PAGE 44, POCKET MAP F6

The **Amstelsluizen** – or Amstel locks – are closed every night when the council begins the process of

De Bazel – The Stadsarchief

sluicing out the canals. A huge pumping station on an island out to the east of the city then starts to pump fresh water from the IJsselmeer into the canal system; similar locks on the west side of the city are left open for the surplus to flow into the IJ and, from there, out to sea. The watery content of the canals is thus regularly refreshed – though, what with all the shopping trolleys and rusty bikes, the water is only appealing as long as you're not actually in it.

The Amstelveld and Reguliersgracht

MAP PAGE 44, POCKET MAP D5

Doubling back from the Amstelsluizen, turn left along the north side of Prinsengracht and you soon reach the **Amstelveld**, where the Monday **flower market** sells flowers and plants, and is much less of a scrum than the Bloemenmarkt. Adjacent **Reguliersgracht** is one of the three surviving radial canals that cut across the Grachtengordel, its dainty humpback bridges and dark waters overlooked by charming seventeenth- and eighteenth-century canal houses.

Rembrandtplein

MAP PAGE 44, POCKET MAP E5

Rembrandtplein may not be Amsterdam at its most alluring, but it is one of the city's nightlife centres, its bevy of restaurants and bars rammed at weekends. Formerly the city's butter market, the square took its present name in 1876 after it had acquired a **statue** of Rembrandt, a rather prim and proper affair that seems particularly appealing to passing seagulls.

The Munttoren and Bloemenmarkt (Flower market)

MAP PAGE 44, POCKET MAP D5

Tiny Muntplein is dominated by the **Munttoren**, an imposing fifteenth-century tower that was once part of the old city wall. Later, the tower was adopted as the municipal mint – hence its name – and in 1620 the celebrated Amsterdam architect Hendrik de Keyser added a flashy spire in what turned out to be one of his last commissions. A few metres away, the floating **Bloemenmarkt**, or **flower market** (daily 9am–5pm, some stalls close on Sun), extends along the southern bank of the Singel. Popular with locals and tourists alike, the market is one of the main suppliers of flowers to central Amsterdam, but its blooms and bulbs now share stall space with souvenir clogs, garden gnomes and similar tat.

Flowers at Bloemenmarkt

Laura Dols

Shops

Architectura & Natura

MAP PAGE 44, POCKET MAP A11
Leliegracht 22. ⓦ architectura.nl.
Outstanding specialist bookshop that more than knows its onions when it comes to architecture, landscape architecture and natural history. Around half of the stock is in English, too.

Boekie Woekie

MAP PAGE 44, POCKET MAP C4
Berenstraat 16. ⓦ boekiewoekie.com.
Sells a good range of books on – and by – leading Dutch artists and graphic designers, with a good-to-great sideline in entertaining postcards: 'Two Lips from Amsterdam', for example.

Brinkman

MAP PAGE 44, POCKET MAP A13
Singel 319.
ⓦ antiquariaatbrinkman.nl.
A stalwart of the Amsterdam antiquarian book trade, Brinkman has lots of good local stuff with expert advice if and when you need it.

Eduard Kramer

MAP PAGE 44, POCKET MAP C6
Prinsengracht 807. ⓦ antique-tileshop.nl.
Large and splendid shop with a charming vintage exterior, where they sell a wonderful selection of Dutch tiles from the fifteenth century onwards; you will, however, be lucky to find a real bargain and, if you are keen to buy a tile or two, you really do need to have done some advance research; the shop also operates an online ordering service.

Episode

MAP PAGE 44, POCKET MAP C4
Berenstraat 1. ⓦ episode.eu.
One of the larger secondhand stores, with everything from army jackets to hats, fur coats, shoes and belts. Specializes in the 1970s and 1980s.

Gerda's Bloemen

MAP PAGE 44, POCKET MAP C4
Runstraat 16. ⓦ gerdasbloemen.com.
Amsterdam is full of flower shops, but this one is the most imaginative. Bouquets to melt the hardest of hearts.

Het Daantje Winkeltje

MAP PAGE 44, POCKET MAP C3

Prinsengracht 228.
A jumble of bargain-basement glassware and crockery, candlesticks, antique tin toys, kitsch souvenirs, old apothecaries' jars, flasks and even clothes too. Perfect for browsing.

De Kaaskamer

MAP PAGE 44, POCKET MAP C4
Runstraat 7. ⓦ kaaskamer.nl.
Friendly shop with a comprehensive selection of Dutch cheeses – much more than ordinary Edam – stacked high up to the rafters. Plus, olives and international wines.

Keren de Vreede Art Gallery

MAP PAGE 44, POCKET MAP C4
Prinsengracht 308A.
ⓦ kerenndevreede.com.
Amsterdam has a brigade of art galleries with art for sale – and this is one of the most diverting. De Vreede displays on her own here in a style that is – for lack of a label – abstract Expressionist. Her paintings are soft, warm and very colourful, built up with thick layers of acrylic paint.

Laura Dols

MAP PAGE 44, POCKET MAP C4
Wolvenstraat 7. ⓦ lauradols.nl.
Superb – and superbly creative – assortment of vintage clothing from dresses through to hats with rails that groan under the weight of countless dresses, all sorted according to colour. Also vintage swimwear, skirts, printed fabrics and tablecloths, though its forte is 1940s and 1950s gear.

Marlies Dekkers

MAP PAGE 44, POCKET MAP C4
Berenstraat 18. ⓦ marliesdekkers.com.
One of Holland's most successful lingerie designers, Dekkers launched her first collection in 1993 to general acclaim from the fashion industry. Her range is sleek and stylish with a good dash of originality and she now has stores all over the Netherlands.

Puccini Bomboni

MAP PAGE 44, POCKET MAP A11
Singel 184. ⓦ puccinibomboni.com.
Without doubt the best chocolatier in town, selling a wonderfully creative range of chocs in all sorts of shapes and sizes – try, for example, the rhubarb and white chocolate ganache encased in dark chocolate; the fig marzipan chocolate; or the cognac ganache consisting of cognac, raisins and cream. This mini-chain has also abandoned the tweeness of the traditional chocolatier for brisk and bright modern decor. There's another outlet in one of the quaintest parts of the city at Staalstraat 17 (see page 36).

Coffeeshops

The Bulldog

MAP PAGE 44, POCKET MAP C5
Leidseplein 17. ⓦ thebulldog.com.
The biggest and arguably the most famous of the coffeeshop chains, and a long way from its poky Red Light District origins. This, the main Leidseplein branch, housed in a former police station, has a cocktail bar, coffeeshop, juice bar and souvenir shop. It's big and brash, not at all the place for a quiet smoke, though the dope they sell (packaged in neat little branded bags) is reliably good.

Grey Area

MAP PAGE 44, POCKET MAP A11
Oude Leliestraat 2. ⓦ greyarea.nl.
No surrender sort of place, a dark and compact little place where the emphasis is on the dope – and the zillions of stickers that adorn every surface in sight. No gentrification here.

Happy Feelings

MAP PAGE 44, POCKET MAP C5
Kerkstraat 51.

The Bulldog

happyfeelingsamsterdam.com. What used to be a hippie hangout, turned into a fresh, trendy and welcoming coffeeshop with flatscreens on the walls, attracting a select clientele.

Siberië

MAP PAGE 44, POCKET MAP B10
Brouwersgracht 11. thecoffeeshops.com. Very relaxed, very friendly, this pleasantly decorated establishment is one of the city's more appealing coffeeshops, with magazines and a chessboard or two.

The OtherSide

MAP PAGE 44, POCKET MAP A14
Reguliersdwarsstraat 6. theotherside.nl. Essentially a LGBTQ+-friendly coffeeshop (in Dutch, "the other side" is a euphemism for being a homosexual), that is straight-friendly and has a fun and welcoming atmosphere.

La Tertulia

MAP PAGE 44, POCKET MAP C4
Prinsengracht 312.
coffeeshoptertulia.com/shop. A very friendly and welcoming coffeeshop – light, bright, and filled with plants – that has held its stellar spot along the canal since 1983. It's the perfect place for women, whether solo or with friends, who might be put off by the atmosphere of other coffeeshops in Amsterdam.

Cafés and tearooms

Buffet van Odette

MAP PAGE 44, POCKET MAP D6
Prinsengracht 598.
buffet-amsterdam.nl. Smart, modern and attractive café serving excellent light meals and salads, plus more substantial meals in the evening. The fresh pasta dishes are especially good. €

Greenwoods

MAP PAGE 44, POCKET MAP B11
Singel 103. greenwoods.eu. Cosy English-style teashop in the basement of a canal house. Pies and sandwiches, pots of tea, traditional cream teas – and a decent breakfast. Very popular so come early(ish) to be sure of a

prime seat either inside or on the pavement patio.

Lanskroon

MAP PAGE 44, POCKET MAP A13
Singel 385. ⓦ lanskroon.nl.
This long-established bakery and tearoom is something of an institution. There's nothing fancy about the decor – though it is homely enough – and there are only a handful of tables, but the bread is reliably good and the cakes and biscuits are simply splendid – the blackcurrant tart is nothing short of magnificent. €

Pompadour

MAP PAGE 44, POCKET MAP C4
Huidenstraat 12. ⓦ pompadour.amsterdam.
This combined tearoom, patisserie and chocolatier has a fancy interior with deluxe wallpaper and oodles of vintage wood panelling. Sells mouth-watering chocolates, cakes and tarts – either eat-in or takeaway. Don't leave without trying one of the raspberry or strawberry mousses. €

Restaurants

De Belhamel

MAP PAGE 44, POCKET MAP B10
Brouwersgracht 60. ⓦ belhamel.nl.
Delightful restaurant, one of the city's best, where the Art Nouveau decor makes for a charming setting and the menu is short but extremely well-chosen, mixing Dutch with French and Italian dishes. One typical dish is the marinated tuna with beetroot, eggplant and sesame dressing. Offers fine canal views from its vantage point on Brouwersgracht. €€€

Beulings

MAP PAGE 44, POCKET MAP A14
Beulingstraat 9. ⓦ beulings.nl.
Intimate restaurant, all white tablecloths and soft lighting, where an inventive Franco–Dutch menu includes such dishes BBQ Pluma Iberica, fava beans, sorrel and tortilla. Three and four-course set menus only. Reservations highly recommended. A good place for a more formal outing – rather than a casual knees-up. €€€€

Brasserie Ambassade

MAP PAGE 44, POCKET MAP A13
Herengracht 339.
ⓦ brasserieambassade.nl.
Sleek, smart and modern restaurant in a handsome old canal house – and a side-line for the excellent and adjacent *Ambassade Hotel* (see page 115). Offers an excellent French-international menu featuring the likes of lobster and beurre noisette or duck with onion, carrot, bacon and potatoes in a red wine jus. €€€

Bussia

MAP PAGE 44, POCKET MAP C3
Reestraat 28. ⓦ bussia.nl.
In the heart of the Grachtengordel, this top-notch Italian restaurant offers a well-chosen menu using only the freshest of ingredients. Everything is home-made, from the original Italian gelato through to the pasta. The lamb-filled ravioli and the slow-cooked lobster in a lobster bisque sauce are both absolutely delicious. Also has an in-house traditional bakery. €€€

Café de Klepel

MAP PAGE 44, POCKET MAP A10
Prinsenstraat 22. ⓦ cafedeklepel.nl.
Long-established brown bar turned into first-rate restaurant, an intimate sort of place serving up delicious French-inspired dishes from a short but finely tuned menu. Nicely located in the Grachtengordel. Three- and four-course set menus. €€€

Chez Georges

MAP PAGE 44, POCKET MAP A11
Herenstraat 3. ⓦ chez-georges.nl.
This much-praised French restaurant offers immaculately presented dishes – try, for example,

the duo of North Sea fish with Roseval potato, lobster *beurre blanc* or even try one of the traditional Belgian main courses on offer – the Gentse Waterzooi (a glorified stew) is simply delicious. The split-level interior, with its somewhat rustic air, adds a certain homely, charm to the place and there's an excellent selection of wines, too, not necessarily at wallet-searing prices. €€€€

Golden Temple

MAP PAGE 44, POCKET MAP E6
Utrechtsestraat 126.
restaurantgoldentemple.com.

Laidback place with a little more soul than the average Amsterdam veggie joint. Inexpensive, well prepared, lacto-vegetarian food with pleasant, attentive service. No alcohol. The florid, broadly Indonesian décor works surprisingly well, too. €

John Dory

MAP PAGE 44, POCKET MAP D6
Prinsengracht 999. johndory.nl.

Occupying a tastefully updated old warehouse on the edge of the Grachtengordel, this canalside restaurant specializes in seafood – both wet-fish and shellfish. It's a smart and fashionable sort of place, where the range of set menus begins at four courses. The décor is brisk and modern with the upper level equipped with white-linen tablecloths set beneath the old roof timbers. Reservations are well-nigh essential. €€€€

Pancake Bakery

MAP PAGE 44, POCKET MAP C2
Prinsengracht 191. pancake.nl.

Located in the basement of an old canal house, this long-established, very informal restaurant offers a mind-boggling range of fillings for its pancakes, both sweet and savoury. There are, for example, pancakes with mushrooms, tomatoes and onions through to (the much more enticing) versions with banana and Nutella or lemon and sugar. A tourist favourite. €

Shiva

MAP PAGE 44, POCKET MAP B14
Reguliersdwarsstraat 72.
shivarestaurant.nl.

Appealing Indian restaurant in trim premises near the Rembrandtplein. Offers a wide-ranging menu covering all the classics, plus a few dishes you might not have tried before. Service is fast and the food is very well presented. €€

Struisvogel

MAP PAGE 44, POCKET MAP C4
Keizersgracht 312.
restaurantdestruisvogel.nl.

This cosy, bistro-style restaurant, in the basement of an old canal house, has a short but imaginative menu with a representative dish being mackerel with beetroot tartare and horseradish mayonnaise. Struisvogel means 'ostrich' in Dutch and this wily bird often appears on the menu too. €€€

Van de Kaart

MAP PAGE 44, POCKET MAP C6

De Belhamel

Prinsengracht 512. ⓦ vandekaart.com. First-rate French/Mediterranean basement restaurant decorated in chic minimalist style and featuring an inventive, ever-changing set menu. The latter showcases such delights as aubergine ravioli with roasted pumpkin and tomato gravy. Reservations well-nigh essential. €€€€

Bars

Arendsnest

MAP PAGE 44, POCKET MAP A11
Herengracht 90. ⓦ arendsnest.nl.
In a handsome old canal house, this bar boasts impressive wooden decor – from the longest of bars to the tall wood-and-glass cabinets – and specializes in Dutch beers, of which it has over 100 varieties, about half of them on draft.

Café Slijterij Oosterling

MAP PAGE 44, POCKET MAP E6
Utrechtsestraat 140. ⓦ cafeoosterling.nl.
Stone-floored, neighbourhood café-cum-bar and off-licence that's long been owned by the same family. Specializes in spirits in general and *jenever* (gin) in particular, with dozens of brands and varieties.

Het Papeneiland

MAP PAGE 44, POCKET MAP C1
Prinsengracht 2. ⓦ papeneiland.nl.
With its wood panelling, antique Delft tiles and ancient stove, this is one of the cosiest bars in the Grachtengordel. It gets packed late at night with a garrulous crew.

De Pieper

MAP PAGE 44, POCKET MAP C5
Prinsengracht 424. ⓣ 020 626 4775.
Relaxed neighbourhood brown bar with rickety old furniture and a terrace beside the canal. Inhabited by a chatty and friendly crew.

De Prins

MAP PAGE 44, POCKET MAP C2
Prinsengracht 124. ⓦ deprins.nl.
This popular and lively brown bar has well-worn decor, live bands and an amiable atmosphere. Also offers a wide range of drinks plus well-priced bar food – sandwiches, salads, burgers and so forth.

Spanjer & van Twist

MAP PAGE 44, POCKET MAP C2
Leliegracht 60. ⓦ spanjerenvantwist.nl.
Hip café-bar with an arty air and modern fittings. Tasty snacks and light bites plus an outside mini-terrace right on the canal. Handy for the Anne Frank Huis (see page 46).

The Waterhole

MAP PAGE 44, POCKET MAP C5
Korte Leidsedwarsstraat 49. ⓦ waterhole.nl.
Late-night bar with live music most nights, anything from punk and rock to jazz and blues. It's especially popular for its regular "new bands" sessions, which attract a raucous but friendly crew; competitively priced beer too.

Weber

MAP PAGE 44, POCKET MAP B5
Marnixstraat 397. ⓦ barweber.nl.
Popular local hangout with ornate and creative furnishings and fittings. Attracts musicians, students and young professionals. Jam packed on the weekend.

Whisky Café L&B

MAP PAGE 44, POCKET MAP C6
Korte Leidsedwarsstraat 82. ⓦ lbwhiskyproeverijen.nl.
Liver--threatening bar with literally hundreds of whiskies to choose from – from Japan to America via Scotland and everywhere in between. Pleasant premises too, cave-like and atmospheric.

Clubs and venues

Escape

MAP PAGE 44, POCKET MAP C14
Rembrandtplein 11. ⓦ escape.nl.

This vast club once hosted Amsterdam's cutting edge Chemistry nights and has an ear-bashing sound system that appeals to mainstream punters.

Jazz Café Alto

MAP PAGE 44, POCKET MAP C5
Korte Leidsedwarsstraat 115.
Ⓦ jazz-cafe-alto.nl.
It's worth hunting down this legendary little jazz bar just off Leidseplein for its quality modern jazz. It's big on atmosphere, though slightly cramped, and entry is usually free.

Jimmy Woo

MAP PAGE 44, POCKET MAP C5
Korte Leidsedwarsstraat 18.
Ⓦ jimmywoo.com.
Intimate and stylish club spread over two floors. Upstairs, the black lacquered walls, Japanese lamps and cosy booths with leather couches ooze sexy chic, while downstairs a packed dance floor throbs under hundreds of oscillating lightbulbs. Popular with young, well-dressed locals, so look smart if you want to join (and get) in.

Melkweg (Milky Way)

MAP PAGE 44, POCKET MAP B5
Lijnbaansgracht 234a. Ⓦ melkweg.nl.
Probably Amsterdam's most famous entertainment venue. A former dairy (hence the name) just round the corner from Leidseplein, this has two separate halls for live music, and puts on a broad range of bands covering everything from reggae to rock, all of which lean towards the "alternative". Excellent DJ sessions go on late at the weekend. There's also a monthly film programme, a theatre, gallery and café-restaurant.

Paradiso

MAP PAGE 44, POCKET MAP C6
Weteringschans 6–8. Ⓦ paradiso.nl.
A converted church near the Leidseplein, revered by many for its excellent programme, featuring local and international bands. Club

Spanjer en van Twist

nights draw in the crowds, and look out also for DJ sets on Fridays and Saturdays. Sometimes hosts classical concerts, as well as debates and multimedia events.

Stadsschouwburg – International Theater Amsterdam

MAP PAGE 44, POCKET MAP B5
Leidseplein 26. Ⓦ ita.nl.
Long-established concert hall in the thick of Amsterdam's nightlife offering a wide range of performances, including theatre, opera and dance by both Dutch and foreign troupes.

Theater Carré

MAP PAGE 44, POCKET MAP F6
Amstel 115–125. Ⓦ carre.nl.
A splendid late-nineteenth-century structure constitutes the ultimate venue for Dutch folk artists, and hosts all kinds of top international acts – anything from Van Morrison to Carmen, with reputable touring orchestras, opera companies and comedy acts squeezed in between. Has a grand setting too, overlooking the River Amstel, near the Magere Brug (see page 51).

The Jordaan and western docklands

On the western side of the city centre, the Jordaan is an area of slender canals and narrow streets flanked by an agreeable mix of modest, modern terraces and handsome seventeenth-century canal houses. It was traditionally the home of Amsterdam's working class, but in recent decades it has become one of the most sought-after residential neighbourhoods in the city. Until the 1970s, the inhabitants were primarily stevedores and factory workers earning a crust in the Scheepvaartsbuurt (Shipping Quarter) that edges the north of the Jordaan. This quarter is now a mixed shopping and residential area, while just beyond, the Westerdok is the oldest and more westerly part of the sprawling complex of artificial islands that sweeps along both sides of the River IJ.

The Jordaan

MAP PAGE 62, POCKET MAP B3

According to dyed-in-the-wool locals, the true Jordaaner is born within earshot of the Westerkerk bells, which means that there are endless arguments as to quite where the district's southern boundary lies, though at least the other borders are clear – Prinsengracht, Brouwersgracht and Lijnbaansgracht. The streets just north of Leidsegracht – often deemed to be the southern border – are routinely modern, though neighbouring **Looiersgracht**, running either side of its canal, does have its scenic moments.

Elandsgracht

MAP PAGE 62, POCKET MAP B4

The narrow streets and canals just to the north of the Looiersgracht are pleasant if unremarkable, but **Elandsgracht** does hold, at no. 109, the enjoyable indoor antiques centre **Antiekcentrum Amsterdam** (see page 64). Football enthusiasts will also want to take a peek at the Smit-Cruyff sports shop at Elandsgracht 98, where **Johan Cruyff** (1947–2016) – star of Ajax in the 1970s and one of the greatest players of all time – bought his first pair of football boots. Nearby, at the east end of Elandsgracht you might pause to look at the **statues** of a handful of Jordaan notables, including **Johnny Jordaan** (1924–89) and **Tante Leen** (1912–92) – two singers who were for years the sound of the working-class Jordaaner, and whose songs are still remembered and sung in some of the area's more raucous cafés.

Rozengracht

MAP PAGE 62, POCKET MAP B3

Rozengracht, a few blocks further north and the area's main artery, slices through the centre of the Jordaan, though this wide street lost most of its character when its canal was filled in and is now a busy main road. It was here, at no. 184, that Rembrandt spent the last ten years of his life in diminished circumstances – a plaque distinguishes his old home.

Bloemgracht

MAP PAGE 62, POCKET MAP B3

The streets and canals between Rozengracht and Westerstraat form the heart of the Jordaan and hold the district's prettiest sights. North of Rozengracht, the first canal is the **Bloemgracht** (Flower Canal), a leafy waterway dotted with houseboats and arched by dinky little bridges, its network of cross-streets sprinkled with cafés, bars and idiosyncratic shops. There's a warm, relaxed community atmosphere here which is really rather beguiling, not to mention a clutch of fine old canal houses. Pride of architectural place goes to **Bloemgracht 87–91**, a sterling Renaissance building of 1642 complete with a trio of distinctive facade stones, representing a *steeman* (city-dweller), a *landman* (farmer) and a *seeman* (sailor). **Nos. 83–85** next door were built a few decades later.

Tulip Museum

MAP PAGE 62, POCKET MAP C2
Prinsengracht 116, at Egelantiersgracht. amsterdamtulipmuseum.com. Charge.
More of a shop than a museum, the **Tulip Museum** sells all sorts of flower-related items upstairs, while down below is a moderately interesting exhibition on the history of the tulip with some details on the speculative bubble in tulip prices that sprouted through the Netherlands in the Golden Age.

Pianola Museum

MAP PAGE 62, POCKET MAP C2
Westerstraat 106. pianola.nl. Charge.
Busy Westerstraat is fairly ordinary, but it's here you'll find the small but charming **Pianola Museum**, which has a collection of **pianolas** and automatic music machines dating from the beginning of the twentieth century, some fifteen of which have been restored to working order. These machines were the jukeboxes of their day, and the museum has a vast collection of over fifteen thousand rolls of music, some of which were "recorded" by famous pianists and composers. It also runs a regular programme of pianola music concerts

Karthuizerhofje

MAP PAGE 62, POCKET MAP B2
Karthuizersstraat 89–171. Free.
Tucked away behind a white doorway, the seventeenth-century **Karthuizerhofje** is the largest of Jordaan's **hofjes** (alms houses). The substantial courtyard complex

Antiekcentrum Amsterdam

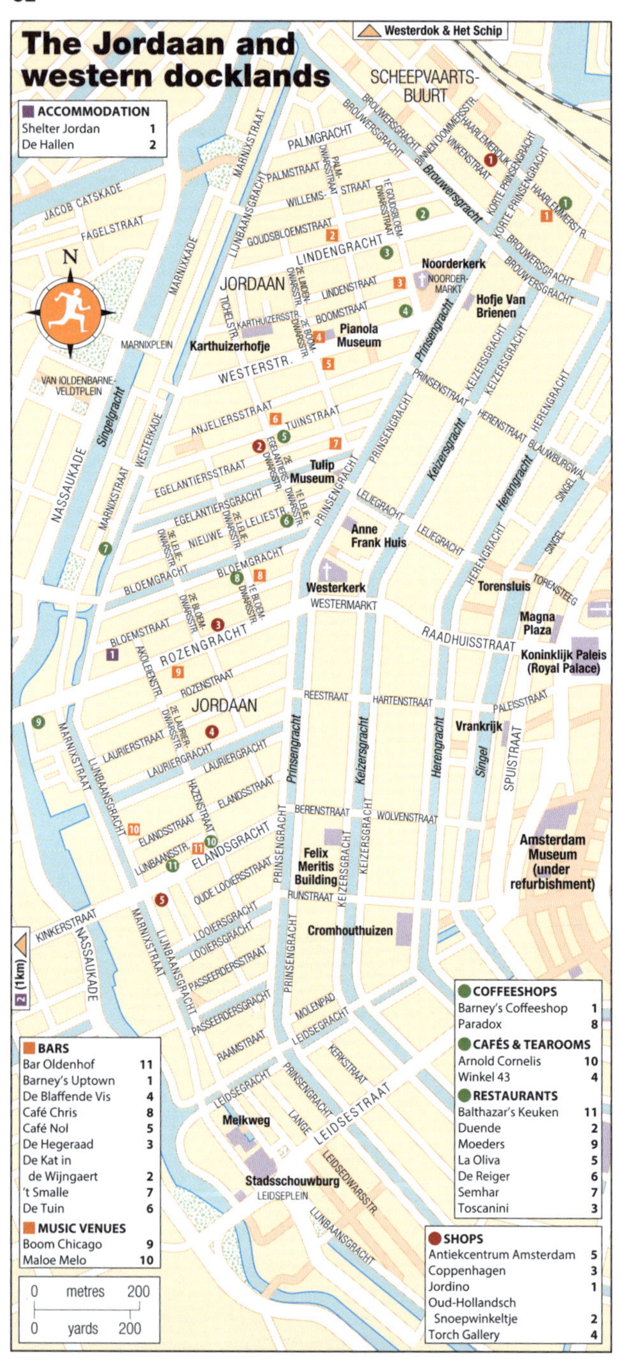

The Jordaan and western docklands
ACCOMMODATION
Shelter Jordan 1
De Hallen 2
BARS
Bar Oldenhof 11
Barney's Uptown 1
De Blaffende Vis 4
Café Chris 8
Café Nol 5
De Hegeraad 3
De Kat in de Wijngaert 2
't Smalle 7
De Tuin 6
MUSIC VENUES
Boom Chicago 9
Maloe Melo 10
COFFEESHOPS
Barney's Coffeeshop 1
Paradox 8
CAFÉS & TEAROOMS
Arnold Cornelis 10
Winkel 43 4
RESTAURANTS
Balthazar's Keuken 11
Duende 2
Moeders 9
La Oliva 5
De Reiger 6
Semhar 7
Toscanini 3
SHOPS
Antiekcentrum Amsterdam 5
Coppenhagen 3
Jordino 1
Oud-Hollandsch Snoepwinkeltje 2
Torch Gallery 4
0 metres 200
0 yards 200
Westerdok & Het Schip
SCHEEPVAARTSBUURT
JORDAAN
Noorderkerk
Hofje Van Brienen
Pianola Museum
Karthuizerhofje
Tulip Museum
Anne Frank Huis
Westerkerk
Torensluis
Magna Plaza
Koninklijk Paleis (Royal Palace)
Vrankrijk
Amsterdam Museum (under refurbishment)
Felix Meritis Building
Cromhouthuizen
Melkweg
Stadsschouwburg
LEIDSEPLEIN
2 (1km)

Westerdok

has picket-fenced gardens and old ornate water-pumps, and makes a peaceful port of call.

Lindengracht

MAP PAGE 62, POCKET MAP C1

Lindengracht (Canal of Limes) lost its waterway decades ago, and is now a quiet and fairly nondescript thoroughfare flanked for the most part by an indeterminate mix of twentieth-century apartment blocks. The east end of Lindengracht intersects with **Brouwersgracht** (see page 42), one of Amsterdam's prettiest streets.

The Scheepvaartsbuurt and the Westerdok

MAP PAGE 62, POCKET MAP C1

Brouwersgracht marks both the northern edge of the Jordaan and the southern boundary of the **Scheepvaartsbuurt** – the Shipping Quarter. In the eighteenth and nineteenth centuries, this Shipping Quarter boomed from its location between the Brouwersgracht and the **Westerdok**, a parcel of land dredged out of the River IJ immediately to the north and equipped with docks, warehouses and shipyards. The Westerdok hung on to some of the marine trade until the 1960s, but today the area is busy reinventing itself, as the old warehouses are turned into apartments. The **Westerpark** provides a spot of green for the locals, and the **Westergas** (westergas.nl), a former gasworks, has been turned into a cultural zone full of design companies and restaurants; it hosts a fashion market on the first Sunday of each month.

Het Schip

MAP PAGE 62, POCKET MAP C1

Visitor Centre: Oostzaanstraat 45. hetschip.nl. Charge.

Tucked away in a rather glum part of the city, **Het Schip** is a municipal housing block comprising a splendid example of the Expressionistic Amsterdam School of architecture. Eight years in the making, from 1913 to 1921, the complex takes its name from its ship-like shape and is graced by all manner of fetching decorative details – from the intriguing mix-and-match windows to the wavy brick facades and ornamental sculptures of which the bulging "cigar" turret is the most self-indulgent. The architect was Michael de Klerk (1884–1923), who was determined to provide high-quality homes for the city's working class. It's an architectural delight - and most of the complex is still used for social housing today.

Shops

Antiekcentrum Amsterdam

MAP PAGE 62, POCKET MAP B4
Elandsgracht 109.
antiekcentrumamsterdam.nl.
This indoor antiques centre is the city's largest with over fifty dealers offering an enormous choice, from vintage watches and jewellery and 1960s ceramics through to ancient furniture and handsomely painted Dutch tiles.

Coppenhagen

MAP PAGE 62, POCKET MAP B3
Rozengracht 54. coppenhagenbeads.nl.
This Jordaan institution stocks beads and beady accessories – including everything you'll need to make your own jewellery. It's a delightfully presented shop too – with oodles of beads displayed by colour and shape.

Jordino

MAP PAGE 62, POCKET MAP D1
Haarlemmerdijk 25a. jordino.nl.
Wonderful chocolate shop and patisserie whose assorted treats crowd an immaculate, partly tiled interior. The chocolates are handmade from the choicest of ingredients, but if it's warm be sure to sample their ice cream, arguably the city's best and in all sorts of favours – pistachio, banana, champagne and so on.

Oud-Hollandsch Snoepwinkeltje

MAP PAGE 62, POCKET MAP C2
Tweede Egelantierdwarsstraat 2.
snoepwinkeltje.com.
Delicious Dutch sweets beaming out from a small army of glass jars in what is very appropriately called the 'Old Dutch Candyshop'. Attract hordes of sweet-tooth kids – so dentists can watch and know their futures are secure.

Torch Gallery

MAP PAGE 62, POCKET MAP B4
Lauriergracht 94. torchgallery.com.
Established in 1984, this is one of the city's most adventurous, sometimes obscurantist, contemporary art galleries. Features several exhibitions every year with Dutch artists to the fore; don't expect any bargains.

Barney's

Coffeeshops

Barney's Coffeeshop

MAP PAGE 62, POCKET MAP D1
Haarlemmerstraat 102.
barneysamsterdam.com.
This popular coffeeshop is a good choice for a spot in town to enjoy a big hit before moving on to *Barney's Uptown* (see page 66) just along the road for a drink.

Paradox

MAP PAGE 62, POCKET MAP B3
1e Bloemdwarsstraat 2.
paradoxcoffeeshop.com.
Paradox satisfies the munchies with outstanding natural food, including spectacular fresh fruit concoctions and veggie burgers. The vibe is laidback and friendly. It also has a particularly good website, including instructions on how to make a space cake.

Cafés and tearooms

Arnold Cornelis

MAP PAGE 62, POCKET MAP B4
Elandsgracht 78. cornelis.nl.
Confectioner and patisserie with a mouthwatering range of pastries and cakes on display behind the most inviting of facades. Take away or eat in the snug tearoom. Try the traditional butter cake if you can't choose – you won't be disappointed. €

Winkel 43

MAP PAGE 62, POCKET MAP C2
Noordermarkt 43. winkel43.nl.
Queue up along with the rest of Amsterdam for Winkel's delectable apple pie –it's home-made daily at this popular lunchroom-cum-restaurant. Some customers claim it's the best apple pie north of the Alps, but they may be exaggerating. Or are they? €

Restaurants

Balthazar's Keuken

MAP PAGE 62, POCKET MAP B4
Elandsgracht 108. balthazarskeuken.nl.
As the name suggests, you feel like you have accidentally stumbled into someone's kitchen here – from the plain and simple tiled walls through to the desserts displayed in the glass cabinets. It's all very engaging and their three-course set menu, which changes every fortnight, is a delightfully imaginative affair featuring such delights as hake with gnocchi, samphire and sea lavender. Reservations required. €€€

Duende

MAP PAGE 62, POCKET MAP C1
Lindengracht 62. cafe-duende.nl.
Busy tapas bar with a partly tiled interior and a warm and inviting feel. Good food and prompt service. There's also a small area that hosts occasional flamenco performances. €€

Moeders

MAP PAGE 62, POCKET MAP B3
Rozengracht 251. moeders.com.
Notably cosy restaurant beside the Singelgracht whose theme is obvious the moment you walk in – mothers, photos of whom plaster the walls. The food is engagingly homespun Dutch grub with the odd modern twist, very tasty and reasonably priced. Try, for example, the 'stampot', a Dutch classic of mashed potatoes with vegetables and sausage. €€

La Oliva

MAP PAGE 62, POCKET MAP C2
Egelantiersstraat 122. laoliva.nl.
Delectable little spot, where they specialize in *pinxtos*, the tasty Basque snacks-on-sticks that make Spanish bar-hopping such a delight. A fine range of Spanish wines provides an excellent accompaniment to round off the meal. €

De Hegeraad

De Reiger

MAP PAGE 62, POCKET MAP C3
Nieuwe Leliestraat 34.
Ⓦ dereigeramsterdam.nl.
In the thick of the Jordaan, this old-style brown café with its vintage furnishings and fittings is jammed with modish Amsterdammers, who enjoy the tasty, traditional Franco–Dutch menu; the oysters are especially good. €

Semhar

MAP PAGE 62, POCKET MAP B3
Marnixstraat 259–261. Ⓦ semhar.nl.
A small, popular and straightforward Ethiopian restaurant with an authentic menu of meat, fish and veggie dishes – all mopped up with a large and spongy flatbread called *injera*. Try the African beer too, which comes served in a *calabash*. €

Toscanini

MAP PAGE 62, POCKET MAP C1
Lindengracht 75. Ⓦ restauranttoscanini.nl.
Big, bustling and authentic Italian restaurant pleasantly lit from its skylight windows. Three-course set menus are the order of the day with great daily specials and an extensive Italian wine list. €€€

Bars

Bar Oldenhof

MAP PAGE 62, POCKET MAP B4
Elandsgracht 84. Ⓦ bar-oldenhof.com.
Lovely,old-fashioned bar with opulent armchairs and subdued lighting. Does a tip-top line in cocktails and single malt whisky; also has an excellent range of wines.

Barney's Uptown

MAP PAGE 62, POCKET MAP D1
Haarlemmerstraat 105.
Ⓦ barneysamsterdam.com.
Pleasant, smoker-friendly bar that's the slick night-time sister of the coffeeshop along the street and with DJs providing a humming backdrop. The American(ish) menu has a choice of burgers, steaks and sandwiches, plus huge breakfasts and weekend brunch.

De Blaffende Vis

MAP PAGE 62, POCKET MAP C2
Westerstraat 118. Ⓣ 020 625 1721.
Something of an institution, this typical neighbourhood bar sits at the corner of the 2e Boomdwarsstraat. Oodles of atmosphere, a well-priced bar menu and a large(ish) pavement terrace.

Café Chris

MAP PAGE 62, POCKET MAP B3
Bloemstraat 42. Ⓦ cafechris.nl.
With good reason, this enjoyable spot is very proud of itself for being the Jordaan's (and Amsterdam's) oldest bar –it dates from 1624. The furnishings and fittings are in the style of a brown café – there are even some stained-glass windows – but there is a pool table too. The atmosphere is homely and convivial

Café Nol

MAP PAGE 62, POCKET MAP C2
Westerstraat 109. Ⓦ cafenol.amsterdam.
Raucous and jolly Jordaan singing bar. This luridly lit dive closes late, especially at weekends, when the back-slapping joviality and drunken sing-alongs (may) keep you rooted until the small hours.

De Hegeraad

MAP PAGE 62, POCKET MAP C2
Noordermarkt 34. Ⓣ 020 624 5565.
Lovingly maintained brown café with a loyal clientele. The vintage-decorated back room is the perfect place to relax with a hot chocolate or, indeed, something stronger.

De Kat in de Wijngaert

MAP PAGE 62, POCKET MAP C1
Lindengracht 160.
Ⓦ dekatindewijngaert.nl.
Complete with a splendid carved sign above its front door, the enticing "Cat in the Vineyard" is the epitome of the Jordaan local with a busy, amiable vibe, bare wooden floors plus jazz on Mondays and Dutch football whenever.

't Smalle

MAP PAGE 62, POCKET MAP C2
Egelantiersgracht 12. Ⓦ t-smalle.nl.
Candlelit and comfortable, this is one of Amsterdam's oldest café-bars sitting pretty beside the canal: it opened in 1786 as a tasting house for the (long-gone) gin distillery next door. Its pavement and pontoon terrace is a perfect spot in summer – arrive early to nab a table.

De Tuin

MAP PAGE 62, POCKET MAP C2
2e Tuindwarsstraat 13. Ⓦ cafedetuin.nl.
The Jordaan has some marvellously unpretentious bars, and this is one of the best: higgledy-piggledy and filled with locals. A well-chosen list of draft guest ales is chalked up behind the bar.

Live music and venues

Boom Chicago

MAP PAGE 62, POCKET MAP B3
Rozengracht 117. Ⓦ boomchicago.nl.
This rapid-fire, English-language improv comedy troupe performs nightly at the Rozentheater to crowds of tourists and locals alike. Comedy festivals, comedy classes and special events too.

Maloe Melo

MAP PAGE 62, POCKET MAP B4
Lijnbaansgracht 163. Ⓦ maloemelo.com.
Dark, low-ceilinged bar, with a back room featuring blues, rock and jazz acts almost every night.

De Tuin

The Old Jewish Quarter and Plantage

The narrow slice of land between the curve of the River Amstel, Oudeschans and the Nieuwe Herengracht was the home of Amsterdam's Jews from the sixteenth century up until World War II. By the 1920s, this Old Jewish Quarter, or Jodenhoek ("Jews' Corner"), was crowded with tenement buildings and smoking factories, its main streets holding scores of open-air stalls selling everything from pickled herrings to pots and pans. The war put paid to all this. In 1945 it lay derelict, and neither has postwar redevelopment treated it kindly; new building has robbed the district of much of its character, but persevere: amid the cars and concrete around Waterlooplein and Mr Visserplein are several moving reminders of the Jewish community that perished in the war, while the neighbouring residential area of Plantage is home to the Artis Zoo and the excellent Verzetsmuseum (Dutch Resistance Museum).

Oudeschans

MAP PAGE 70, POCKET MAP D13
Metro Nieuwmarkt.

Wide and windy, the **Oudeschans** canal began life as Amsterdam's eastern moat until its original function was usurped when more land was dredged out of the River IJ. Thereafter, the Oudeschans was home to a string of shipyards and, although these are long gone, the canal's defensive origins are still recalled by the **Montelbaanstoren**, a sturdy and conspicuous brick tower built in 1516. The tower's decorative spire was added later, when the city felt more secure, to a design by Hendrick de Keyser (1565–1621), the architect who did much to create Amsterdam's prickly skyline.

Rembrandthuis

MAP PAGE 70, POCKET MAP D13
Jodenbreestraat 4. Ⓦ rembrandthuis.nl. Charge.

Once the centre of Jewish life, Jodenbreestraat, the "Broad Street of the Jews", is short on charm, but it is home to the **Rembrandthuis**, whose intricate facade is decorated with pretty wooden shutters. Rembrandt bought this house at the height of his fame and popularity, living here for over twenty years and spending a fortune on furnishings – an expense that ultimately contributed to his bankruptcy. An inventory made at the time details the huge collection of paintings, sculptures and art treasures he had amassed, almost all of which was auctioned off after he was declared insolvent and forced to move to a more modest house in the Jordaan in 1658.

The city council bought the Jodenbreestraat house in 1907 and has revamped the premises on several occasions. A visit begins in the modern building next door, but you're soon into the string of period rooms that have been returned to something like their appearance when Rembrandt lived here, with the original inventory as a guide. The period furniture is enjoyable enough, especially the box beds, and the great man's studio is surprisingly large and well-lit, but it's the collection of seventeenth-century Dutch paintings that grabs most of the attention, notably several works by Rembrandt's master in Amsterdam, Pieter Lastman. On the same floor, in the **Salon**, is the museum's one and only Rembrandt, his *Portrait of the Preacher Eleazer Swalmius*, an early work currently on long-term loan from Antwerp. Beyond is the intriguing "**Art Cabinet**", a room crammed with objets d'art and miscellaneous curios including African spears and Pacific seashells. Beyond the Art Cabinet, the rest of the Rembrandthuis is usually given over to temporary exhibitions on the artist and his contemporaries. There's also, space permitting, a substantial assortment of Rembrandt's **etchings**, as well as several of the original copper plates on which he worked.

Gassan Diamonds

MAP PAGE 70, POCKET MAP D13
Nieuwe Uilenburgerstraat 173. Ⓦ gassan.com. Free; no advance booking required.

Gassan Diamonds occupies a large and imposing brick building dating from 1897. Before World War II, many local Jews worked as diamond cutters and polishers, but there's little sign of the industry hereabouts today, this factory being the main exception. Tours include a visit to the cutting and polishing areas, as well a gambol round Gassan's diamond jewellery showroom.

Stopera – Stadhuis & Muziektheater

MAP PAGE 70, POCKET MAP D14
Amstel 3. Ⓦ operaballet.nl.

Jodenbreestraat runs parallel to the **Stopera – Stadhuis & Muziektheater**, a sprawling and distinctly underwhelming modern complex dating from the 1980s and incorporating the city hall and a large auditorium, the Muziektheater, now rebranded as the **Nationale Opera & Ballet**. The latter offers a varied programme of theatre, dance and ballet as well as opera from the country's first-rate Netherlands Opera (De Nederlandse Opera; Ⓦ operaballet.nl), but tickets go very quickly. One of the city's

Rembrandthuis

A sparkling Gassan diamond

abiding ironies is that the title of the protest campaign aiming to prevent the development in the 1980s – “Stopera” – has passed into common usage to describe the finished complex.

Waterlooplein

MAP PAGE 70, POCKET MAP C14–D14

The indeterminate modernity of the Stopera complex dominates **Waterlooplein**, a rectangular parcel of land that was originally swampy marsh. This was the site of the first Jewish Quarter, but by the late nineteenth century it had become an insanitary slum. The slums were cleared in the 1880s and thereafter the open spaces of the Waterlooplein hosted the largest and liveliest market in the city, the place where Jews and Gentiles met to trade. In the war, the Germans used the square to round up their victims, but despite these ugly connotations the Waterlooplein was revived in the 1950s as the site of the city's main **flea market** (Mon–Sat 9am–5pm) and remains

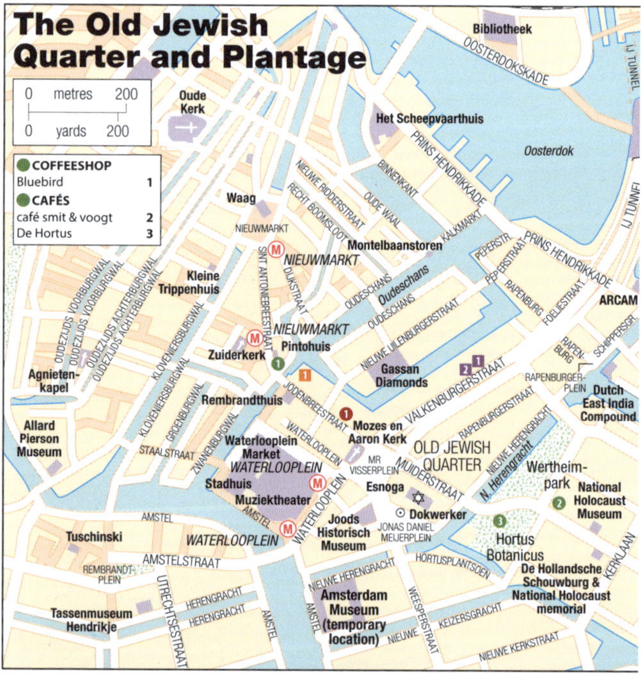

The Old Jewish Quarter and Plantage

0 metres 200
0 yards 200

COFFEESHOP
Bluebird 1
CAFÉS
café smit & voogt 2
De Hortus 3

so to this day. The market is nowhere near as large as it once was, but nonetheless it's still the final resting place of many a pair of yellow corduroy flares and has some diverting antique and junk stalls to root through. If you're after a bargain, head there early, as it's very popular with tourists.

Nearby, at the very tip of Waterlooplein, where the River Amstel meets the Zwanenburgwal canal, there is a sombre **memorial** – a black stone tribute to the dead of the Jewish resistance. The inscription from Jeremiah translates, "If my eyes were a well of tears, I would cry day and night for the fallen fighters of my beloved people." Metres away, a second sculpture honours philosopher and theologian **Baruch Spinoza** who was born nearby in 1632. Of Sephardic descent, Spinoza's pantheistic views soon brought him into conflict with the elders of the Jewish community. At the age of 23, he was excommunicated and forced out of the city, moving into a small village where he survived by grinding lenses. After an attempt on his life, Spinoza moved again, eventually ending up in The Hague, where his freethinking ways proved more acceptable.

Mr Visserplein

MAP PAGE 70, POCKET MAP D14

Just behind the Muziektheater, on the corner of **Mr Visserplein**, is the **Mozes en Aaron Kerk**, a rather glum Neoclassical structure built on the site of a clandestine Catholic church in the 1840s. The square itself, a busy junction for traffic speeding towards the IJ tunnel, takes its name from Mr Visser, President of the Supreme Court of the Netherlands in 1939. He was dismissed the following year when the Germans occupied the country, and became an active member of

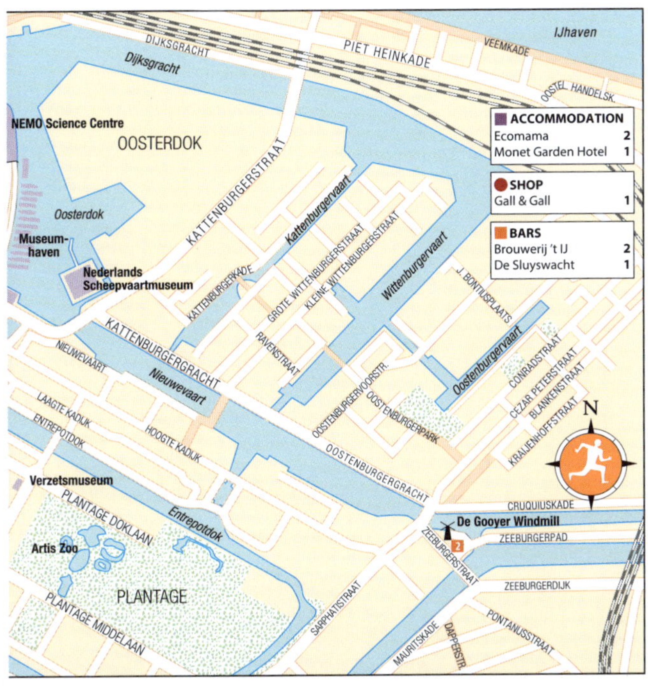

The Esnoga

the Jewish resistance, working for the illegal underground newspaper *Het Parool* ("The Password") and refusing to wear the yellow Star of David. He died in 1942, a few days after publicly – and famously – denouncing all forms of collaboration.

Esnoga

MAP PAGE 70, POCKET MAP D14
Mr Visserplein 3. Ⓦ esnoga.com or Ⓦ jck.nl. Charge, including Joods Historich Museum, Hollandsche Schouwburg and National Holocaust Museum.

The brown and bulky brickwork of the **Esnoga** - or Portuguese synagogue - was completed in 1675 for the city's Sephardic community. One of Amsterdam's most imposing buildings, it has been barely altered since its construction, its lofty interior following the Sephardic tradition in having the *Hechal* (the Ark of the Covenant) and *tebah* (from where services are led) at opposite ends. Also traditional is the seating, with two sets of wooden benches (for the men) facing each other across the central aisle – the women have separate galleries up above. A set of superb brass chandeliers holds the candles that remain the only source of artificial light. When it was completed, the synagogue was one of the largest in the world, its congregation almost certainly the richest; today, the Sephardic community has dwindled to just a few families, whose traditions are celebrated in the surrounding outhouses, from the mourning room to the rabbi's room and the intimate winter synagogue. The mystery is why the Nazis left the building alone – no one knows for sure, but it seems likely that they intended to turn it into a museum once all the Jews had been murdered.

Jonas Daniel Meijerplein

MAP PAGE 70, POCKET MAP F5

In the shadow of the Esnoga, **Jonas Daniel Meijerplein** is the square where, in February 1941, around four hundred Jewish men were loaded onto trucks and taken to their deaths at Mauthausen concentration camp, in reprisal for the killing of a Dutch Nazi during a street fight. The arrests sparked off the February Strike, a general strike in protest against the Germans' treatment of the Jews. It was organized by the outlawed Communist Party and spearheaded by Amsterdam's transport workers and dockers in a rare demonstration of solidarity with the Jews. The strike was quickly suppressed, but is still commemorated by an annual wreath-laying ceremony on February 25, as well as by Mari Andriessen's statue *The Dokwerker* (Dockworker) standing on the square.

Joods Historisch Museum

MAP PAGE 70, POCKET MAP D14

Nieuwe Amstelstraat 1. ⓦ jck.nl. Charge, including Esnoga, Hollandsche Schouwburg and National Holocaust Museum.

The **Joods Historisch Museum** (Jewish Historical Museum) is cleverly shoehorned into four adjacent Ashkenazi synagogues that date from the late seventeenth century. For years after World War II these buildings lay abandoned, but they were finally refurbished – and connected by walkways – in the 1980s, to accommodate a Jewish exhibition centre.

The first major display area, just beyond the reception desk on the ground floor of the Nieuwe Synagoge, features temporary exhibitions on Jewish life and culture. Upstairs is a history of Dutch Jewry from 1900 to the present. Inevitably, the emphasis is on the calamity that befell them during the German occupation of World War II, but there is also a biting display on the indifferent/hostile reaction of many Dutch men and women to liberated Jews in 1945. Moving on, the ground floor of the adjacent **Grote Synagoge** holds an engaging display on Jewish culture. There is a fine collection of religious silverware here, plus all manner of antique artefacts illustrating religious customs and practices. The gallery up above holds a finely judged social history of the country's Jewish population from 1600 to 1900.

Hermitage Amsterdam

MAP PAGE 70, POCKET MAP F5

Amstel 51. ⓦ hermitage.nl. Charge. Note that whilst it's closed for refurbishment, part of the Amsterdam Museum's collection (see page 35) will be displayed here.

The Joods Historisch Museum

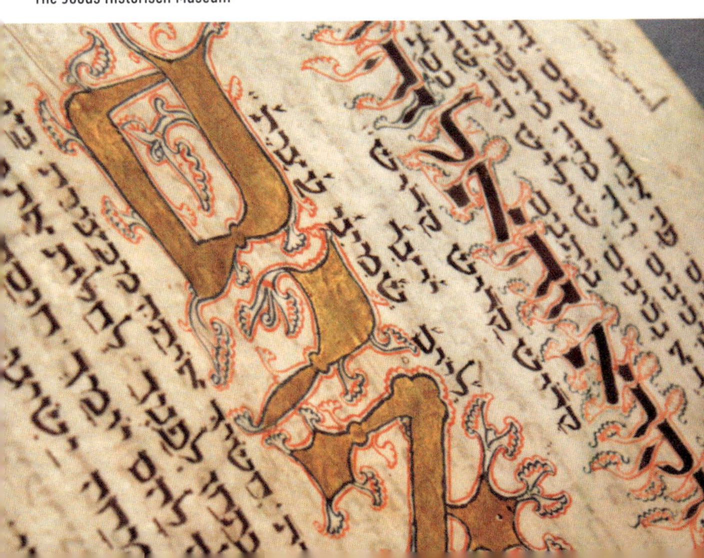

Backing onto the River Amstel, the stern-looking **Amstelhof** started out as a *hofje* or almshouse for the care of elderly women, built in the 1680s on behalf of the Dutch Reformed Church. In time, it grew to fill most of the land between Nieuwe Herengracht and Nieuwe Keizersgracht, becoming a fully fledged hospital in the process, but in the 1980s it became clear that its medical facilities were out of date and it went up for sale. An ambitious scheme ensued to convert it into a museum, the **Hermitage Amsterdam**. With the historic exterior preserved and a light, modern interior, its multiple galleries displayed prime pieces loaned from the Hermitage in St Petersburg – until, that is, Russia's invasion of Ukraine prompted a quick change of tack in March 2022. Exhibitions had included, for example, Spanish Masters from the Hermitage and The Romanovs, but after the break with the Russians, the first show was the widely praised *Dutch Heritage: Amsterdam*. At least the gallery had a head start with its reinvention: even before Ukraine, they had begun to diversify, opening a new section called "Outsider Art Museum" – outsiders being untrained artists, often from psychiatric hospitals and the like.

Plantage

MAP PAGE 70, POCKET MAP G5-H5

Developed in the middle of the nineteenth century, the **Plantage**, with its comfortable streets spreading to either side of the Plantage Middenlaan boulevard, was built as part of a concerted attempt to provide good-quality housing for the city's expanding middle classes. Although it was never as fashionable as the older residential parts of the Grachtengordel (see page 42), the new district did contain elegant villas and spacious terraces, making it a first suburban port of call for many aspiring Jews. Nowadays, the Plantage is still one of the more prosperous parts of the city, in a modest sort of way, and boasts two especially enjoyable attractions – the Hortus Botanicus botanical gardens and the Verzetsmuseum (Dutch Resistance Museum).

Hortus Botanicus

MAP PAGE 70, POCKET MAP F5-G4

Hortus Botanicus

Plantage Middenlaan 2a. dehortus.nl. Charge.
Amsterdam's lush **Hortus Botanicus** was founded in 1682 as medicinal gardens for the use of the city's physicians and apothecaries. Thereafter, many of the city's merchants made a point of bringing back exotic species from the East, the result being the six thousand-odd plant species exhibited here today. The gardens are divided into several distinct sections, each clearly labelled and its location pinpointed by a map available at the entrance kiosk.

Most of the outdoor sections are covered by plants, trees and shrubs from the temperate and Arctic zones. There's also a three-climates glasshouse, where the plants are arranged according to their geographical origins, a capacious palm house, an orchid nursery and a butterfly house. It's all very low-key – and none the worse for that – and the gardens make a relaxing break on any tour of central Amsterdam, especially as the café, in the old orangery, serves up tasty sandwiches, coffee and cakes.

Wertheimpark

MAP PAGE 70, POCKET MAP G4

The pocket-sized **Wertheimpark**, across the road from the Hortus Botanicus, is home to the Auschwitz Monument, a simple affair with symbolically broken mirrors and an inscription that reads *Nooit meer Auschwitz* ("Auschwitz – Never Again"). It was designed by the late Dutch writer, sculptor and painter Jan Wolkers (1925–2007).

National Holocaust Museum

MAP PAGE 70, POCKET MAP G5

Plantage Middenlaan 27. jck.nl. Charge, including Joods Historich Museum, Esnoga and Hollandsche Schouwburg.

The **National Holocaust Museum** occupies a former teacher's training college in the heart of the Plantage. It's an appropriate location as this was the spot where Resistance workers did their best to smuggle out children who had been consigned to the neighbouring De Hollandsche Schouwburg (see page 75) during World War II. The museum presents a wide range of temporary and semi-permanent exhibitions that delve deep into the personal histories of the victims of the Holocaust, focusing on the Netherlands, but setting the disaster into its international context too. The museum continues inside the De Hollandsche Schouwburg.

De Hollandsche Schouwburg

MAP PAGE 70, POCKET MAP G5

Plantage Middenlaan 24. jck.nl. Charge, including Joods Historich Museum, Esnoga and National Holocaust Museum.

Another sad relic of the war, **De Hollandsche Schouwburg** was once a thriving Jewish theatre, but the Germans turned it into the main assembly point for Amsterdam Jews prior to their deportation. Inside, there was no daylight and families were interned in conditions that foreshadowed those of the camps they would soon be transported to. Imaginatively, the old auditorium out at the back has been left as an empty, roofless shell with the addition of a memorial column of basalt on a Star of David base – the **National Holocaust Memorial**. This stands where the stage once was and is an intensely mournful monument to suffering of unfathomable proportions. The front of the building is currently being refurbished to house part of the **National Holocaust Museum** (see page 75), zeroing in on the plight of the city's Jews.

Artis Zoo

MAP PAGE 70, POCKET MAP G5

Plantage Kerklaan 38–40. artis.nl. Charge.

Opened in 1838, **Artis Zoo** is the oldest zoo in the Netherlands and one of the city's top tourist attractions, though thankfully its layout and refreshing lack of bars and cages mean that it never feels overcrowded. Highlights include an African savanna environment, a seventy-metre-long aviary, aquaria and a South American zone with llamas and the world's largest rodent, the capybara. Feeding times, which are always popular, include those for the birds of prey, the seals and sea lions, the pelicans, the penguins, the lions and tigers, and the crocodiles, though these only require a weekly feed. In addition, **Micropia** (extra charge) is dedicated to the secret world of micro-organisms and will appeal to budding biologists. The on-site **Planetarium** (no extra charge) has several shows daily, all in Dutch, though you can pick up a leaflet with an English translation from the desk.

There are also the lovely, manicured zoo gardens which are worth a stroll around in.

Verzetsmuseum

MAP PAGE 70, POCKET MAP G5
Plantage Kerklaan 61.
verzetsmuseum.org. Charge.

The excellent **Verzetsmuseum** (Dutch Resistance Museum) outlines the development of the Dutch Resistance from the German invasion of the Netherlands in May 1940 to the country's liberation in 1945. The main themes of the occupation are dealt with honestly, noting the fine balance between cooperation and collaboration, while smaller displays focus on aspects such as the protest against the rounding-up of Amsterdam's Jews in 1941 and the so-called Milk Strike of 1943. There are fascinating old photographs and a host of original artefacts including examples of illegal newsletters and, chillingly, signed German death warrants. The museum also has dozens of little metal sheets providing biographical sketches of the members of the Resistance.

Verzetsmuseum

Shop

Gall & Gall

MAP PAGE 70, POCKET MAP D13
Jodenbreestraat 23. gall.nl.
Has an outstanding range of Dutch jenevers (gins) and flavoured spirits as well as a good selection of imported wine, champagne and prosecco. Part of the largest chain of wine merchants in Amsterdam.

Coffeshop

Bluebird

MAP PAGE 70, POCKET MAP D13
Sint Antoniesbreestraat 71.
Popular coffeeshop with sink-in sofas and tall stools. The *Bluebird* also serves food, coffees and other non-alcoholic drinks. Very handy for the Rembrandthuis (see page 69).

Cafés

café smit & voogt

MAP PAGE 70, POCKET MAP G5
Plantage Parklaan 10.
cafesmitenvoogt.nl.
A friendly, casual spot serving up great breakfast and lunch. Grab a table outside and round out the meal with a nice big slice of apple pie. €

De Hortus

MAP PAGE 70, POCKET MAP F5
Plantage Middenlaan 2a. dehortus.nl.
Tucked away amid the luxuriant greenery of the Hortus Botanicus (see page 75), this family-orientated café occupies a spacious former orangery. They serve up good, tangy coffee, filling sandwiches and freshly made rolls. But, whatever you do, save space for the desserts in general and the cheesecake in particular: the raspberry cheesecake may well be the best north of the Alps. €

De Hortus

Bars

Brouwerij 't IJ

MAP PAGE 70, POCKET MAP H5
De Gooyer windmill, Funenkade 7.
brouwerijhetij.nl.
Well-established bar and mini-brewery in the old public baths adjoining the De Gooyer windmill. Serves up an excellent range of beers and ales, from the thunderously strong Columbus amber ale (9%) to the creamier, more soothing Natte (6.5%).

De Sluyswacht

MAP PAGE 70, POCKET MAP D13
Jodenbreestraat 1. sluyswacht.nl.
This pleasant little bar occupies an old and now solitary gabled house by the lock gates opposite the Rembrandthuis. A smashing spot to nurse a beer on a warm summer's night, gazing down the canal towards the Montelbaanstoren.

The eastern docklands and Amsterdam Noord

Amsterdam's docklands once extended right along the south side of the River IJ, comprising a vast maritime complex incorporating both the Westerdok (western docklands, see page 63) and the Oosterdok (eastern docklands). Industrial decline began during the 1880s, but the docklands' assorted artificial islands are now being redefined as residential and leisure districts with some startling modern architecture – balanced by two reminders of the Oosterdok's nautical heyday, the warehouses of Entrepotdok and the engaging Scheepvaartmuseum (Maritime Museum). On the north side of the River IJ, and reached by ferry, the former shipyards and commercial buildings of Amsterdam Noord, are in an earlier phase of redevelopment, but the slab of land opposite Centraal Station has been transformed by the construction of the Eye Film Institute, Amsterdam's best cinema in the city's proudest new building. Further out along the north side of the river, there's a second patch of cutting-edge regeneration in the former NDSM Shipyard, now a creative arts and events hub.

Oosterdok

MAP PAGE 80, POCKET MAP H3-4

Stretching east from Centraal Station lies the **Oosterdok**, or **eastern docklands**, whose network of artificial islands was dredged out of the River IJ to increase Amsterdam's shipping facilities in the seventeenth and eighteenth centuries. By the 1980s, this mosaic of docks, jetties and islands had become something of a post-industrial eyesore, but since then an ambitious redevelopment programme has turned things around.

Easily the most agreeable way of reaching the Oosterdok is via the footbridge at the north end of Plantage Kerklaan – and metres from the Verzetsmuseum (see page 76) – which leads onto Entrepotdok.

Entrepotdok

MAP PAGE 80, POCKET MAP G4-5

Over the footbridge at the end of Plantage Kerklaan lies one of the more interesting of the Oosterdok islands, a slender rectangle whose southern quayside, **Entrepotdok**, is lined by a long series of nineteenth-century gabled warehouses that were once part of the largest warehouse complex in continental Europe. Each warehouse sports the name of a town or island; goods for onward transportation were stored in the appropriate warehouse until there were enough to fill a boat or barge. The warehouses have been converted into offices and apartments, a fate that must surely befall the buildings of the central East India Company compound, at the west end of Entrepotdok on Kadijksplein.

Oosterdok

Scheepvaartmuseum

MAP PAGE 80, POCKET MAP G4
Kattenburgerplein.
Ⓦ hetscheepvaartmuseum.nl. Charge.

One of the city's most popular attractions, the **Scheepvaartmuseum** (Maritime Museum) occupies the old arsenal of the Dutch navy, a vast sandstone structure built on the Oosterdok in the seventeenth century. Visitors get their bearings in the central **courtyard** from where you can enter any one of three display areas – labelled "West", "Noord" and "Oost". Of the three, the **West** displays are the most child-orientated, the **Oost** the most substantial, including garish ships' figureheads, examples of early atlases and navigational equipment. There are many nautical paintings in this section too, some devoted to the achievements of Dutch trading ships, others showing heavy seas and shipwrecks and yet more celebrating the successes of the Dutch navy, the most powerful fleet in the world from the 1650s to the 1680s. Willem van de Velde II (1633–1707) was the most successful of the Dutch marine painters of the period and there's a small sample of his work here.

The "**Noord**" section features a couple of short nautical films and also gives access to the 78-metre De Amsterdam, a full-scale replica of an East Indiaman merchant ship. The original vessel first set sail in 1748, but came to an ignominious end, getting stuck on the English coast near Hastings. Visitors can wander the ship's decks, galleys, storerooms and gun bays at their leisure.

ARCAM

MAP PAGE 80, POCKET MAP G4
Prins Hendrikkade 600. Ⓦ arcam.nl. Charge.

Sitting pretty on the waterfront, **ARCAM**, the Amsterdam Centre for Architecture, is housed in a distinctive aluminium and glass structure designed by the Dutch architect René van Zuuk. The design was much praised at the time of its construction, but the building does look rather disconcertingly like the head of a golf club. Inside, a small glass area is used for an imaginative programme of temporary exhibitions on

NEMO Science Museum

contemporary architecture in general and future building plans for Amsterdam in particular. ARCAM also publishes a number of specialist architectural books, maps and leaflets on Amsterdam, and these are on sale here too.

Museumhaven

MAP PAGE 80, POCKET MAP G3
Oosterdok. Free.

Moored on the long jetty leading up to the giant green hood above the IJ tunnel are the antique boats and barges of the **Museumhaven**, which together make an informal record of the development of local shipping; the earliest boats date from the middle of the nineteenth century, and plaques, in English and Dutch, give the historical lowdown on the more important vessels.

NEMO Science Museum

MAP PAGE 80, POCKET MAP G3
Oosterdok. Ⓦ nemosciencemuseum.nl.

Charge.

Much of the distinctive elevated hood above the IJ tunnel is occupied by NEMO, a (pre-teenage) kids' attraction par excellence, with all sorts of interactive science and technological exhibits spread over six floors and set out under several broad themes. You can book activities on their website such as hands-on chemistry experiments and learning what it takes to be an inventor.

There's also a sustainable restaurant on the roof designed by architect Renzo Piano with breathtaking panoramic views. You can also explore the piazza on the roof with open-air exhibitions on sustainable energy and interactive sculptures exploring energy captured from wind, water and sun.

Bibliotheek

MAP PAGE 80, POCKET MAP F2

Oosterdokskade 143. Ⓦ oba.nl. Free.

Across the harbour-spanning footbridge from NEMO, Amsterdam's principal **Bibliotheek** (Library) occupies a cleverly designed modern block that was opened in 2007. The building was designed by Jo Coenon, a Dutch architect and urban planner of repute, and the spacious, subtly lit interior spreads over ten floors; among much else, it includes an auditorium, an exhibition room and a terrace café, which is a popular spot for students to chew the academic cud.

Muziekgebouw aan 't ij

MAP PAGE 80, POCKET MAP G2

Piet Heinkade 1 Ⓦ muziekgebouw.nl.

One of the Oosterdok's prime buildings, the **Muziekgebouw** is a high-spec, multipurpose music auditorium overlooking the River IJ. It encompasses two medium-

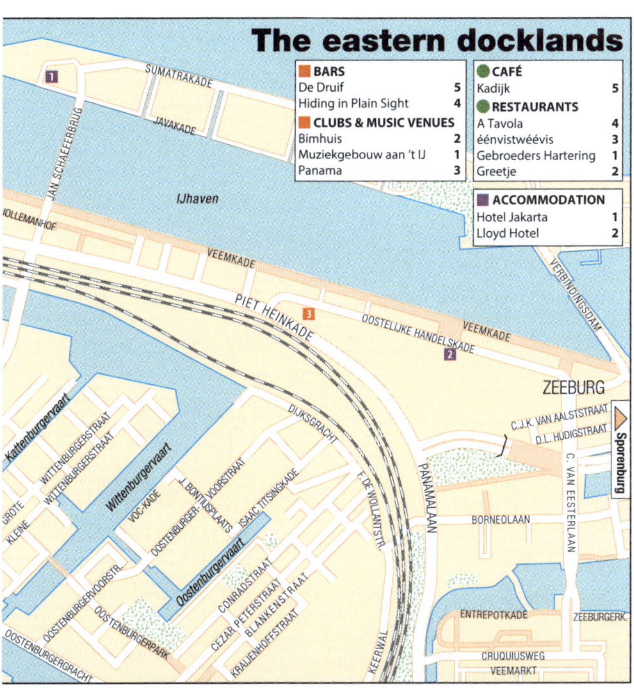

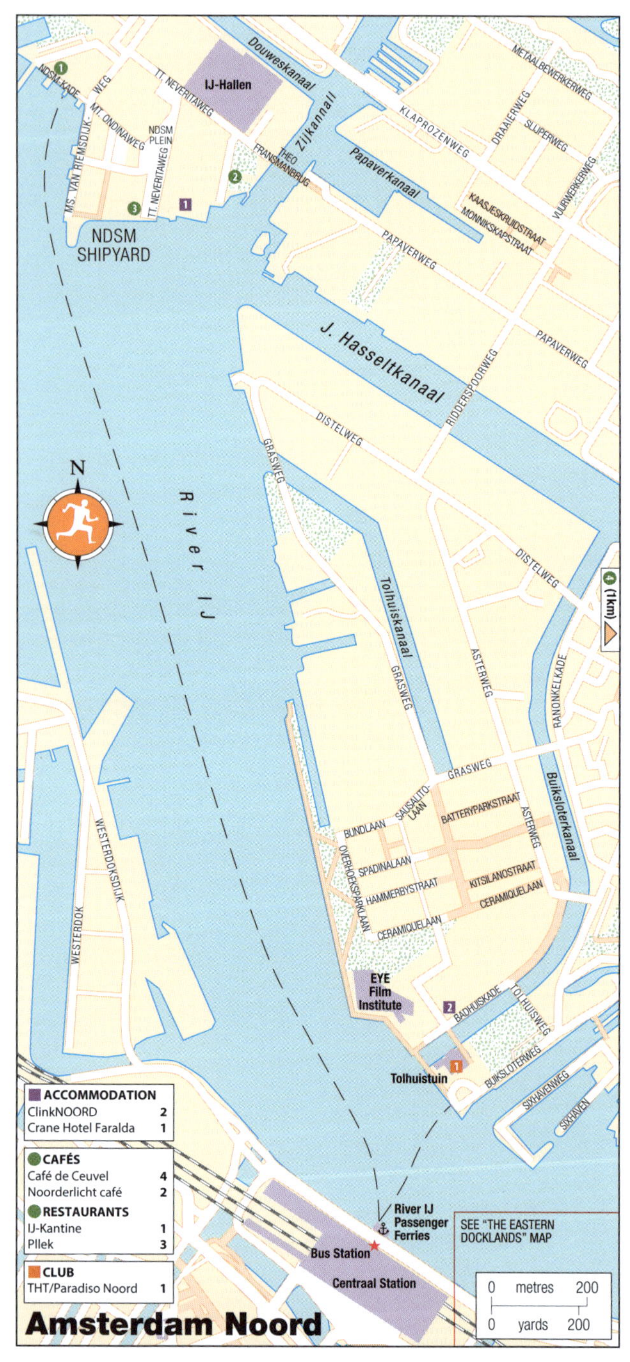
Amsterdam Noord
ACCOMMODATION
ClinkNOORD 2
Crane Hotel Faralda 1
CAFÉS
Café de Ceuvel 4
Noorderlicht café 2
RESTAURANTS
IJ-Kantine 1
Pllek 3
CLUB
THT/Paradiso Noord 1
IJ-Hallen
NDSM SHIPYARD
NDSM PLEIN
NDSM-KADE
MT. ONDINAWEG
TT. NEVERITAWEG
MS. VAN RIEMSDIJK-WEG
THEO FRANSMANBRUG
Douweskanaal
Zijkanaal I
Papaverkanaal
KLAPROZENWEG
METAALBEWERKERWEG
DRAAIERWEG
SLIJPERWEG
VUURWERKERWEG
KAASJESKRUIDSTRAAT
MONNIKSKAPSTRAAT
PAPAVERWEG
J. Hasseltkanaal
RIDDERSPOORWEG
DISTELWEG
GRASWEG
River IJ
Tolhuiskanaal
ASTERWEG
RANONKELKADE
Buiksloterkanaal
WESTERDOKSDIJK
WESTERDOK
SAUSALITO-LAAN
BATTERYPARKSTRAAT
BUNDLAAN
SPADINALAAN
OVERHOEKSPARKLAAN
HAMMERBYSTRAAT
KITSILANOSTRAAT
CERAMIQUELAAN
EYE Film Institute
BADHUISKADE
TOLHUISWEG
BUIKSLOTERWEG
Tolhuistuin
SIXHAVENWEG
SIXHAVEN
River IJ Passenger Ferries
Bus Station
Centraal Station
SEE "THE EASTERN DOCKLANDS" MAP
(1km)
0 metres 200
0 yards 200
N

sized concert halls, a café and a bar. It also has state-of-the-art acoustics, and has given real impetus to the redevelopment going on along the IJ. As well as some contemporary music, it has a good programme of opera and orchestral music which brings a rather highbrow crowd to this part of town. It's worth a visit for the building alone.

Zeeburg

MAP PAGE 80, POCKET MAP H5

To the east of the Muziekgebouw lies **Zeeburg** – basically the old docklands stretching out as far as **Java** and KNSM islands and today one of the city's most up-and-coming districts. Actually a series of artificial islands and peninsulas connected by bridges, the docks here date to the end of the nineteenth century. By the early 1990s, the area was virtually derelict, so the council began a massive renovation, which has been going on for nearly two decades. This is now the fastest-developing part of Amsterdam, with a mixture of renovated dockside structures and new landmark buildings that give it a modern (and very watery) feel that's markedly different from the city centre – despite being just a ten-minute walk from Centraal Station. Explore the area by **bike**, especially as distances are, at least in Amsterdam terms, comparatively large – from the Muziekgebouw to the east end of KNSM Island is about 4km.

Alternatively, there are two useful transport connections from Centraal Station: tram #26 along Piet Heinkade to Sporenburg and bus #43 to Java Island and KNSM Island.

EYE Film Institute

MAP PAGE 82. POCKET MAP E1

IJpromenade 1. ⓦ eyefilm.nl.

Clearly visible from the south side of the River IJ, the **EYE Film Institute** occupies a superb new building, a graceful shimmering structure whose sleek, angular

Zeeburg

lines were designed by a Viennese architecture company, Delugan Meissl. The EYE offers engaging views back over both the river and the city centre from all its three floors, which hold a bar-restaurant, a shop, a film-focused library and four cinema screens showing an enterprising programme of classic and cult films. There is also an exhibition area offering four major displays each year.

NDSM Shipyard

MAP PAGE 82, POCKET MAP E1

Free.

Until it closed in 1979, the **NDSM Shipyard** was a key part of Amsterdam's industrial economy, its workshops, wharves and engineering plant spreading over a large chunk of land on the north side of the River IJ. After NDSM's demise, no one was quite sure what to do with the site, but very little was demolished. The first band of incomers after the shipyard's closure brought an eco-New Age vibe to the area: several of the old distressed industrial buildings and shipping containers were refitted and an old Soviet submarine was moored in the harbor, though plans to turn this into a party venue never worked out. The submarine is still there – as is a Greenpeace ship – but the graffiti on the sub – 'f**k gentrification' - seems something of a forlorn hope: the arrival of the conspicuous – and conspicuously mundane – *DoubleTree by Hilton Hotel* does not augur well. The main sight as such is the cavernous **IJ-Hallen** (ⓦ ijhallen.nl/en/), which comes complete with a number of massive industrial fittings recalling the days it was the heart of the shipyard. Nowadays, the IJ-Hallen is used for a variety of events, including regular flea markets, while the recycled buildings nearby form a fashionable arts and events hub and hold several boho clubs and restaurants.

Street art at the NDSM Shipyard

Greetje

Cafés

Café de Ceuvel

MAP PAGE 82, POCKET MAP F1

Korte Papaverweg 4. deceuvel.nl.

Well off the beaten track, about thirty minutes' walk north of the Eye Film Institute, this vegetarian highlight occupies part of an old shipyard that has been reclaimed and revitalised in full eco style. The café is a lively and informal affair serving light bites, great quiches and fabulous homemade lemonade. €

Kadijk

MAP PAGE 80, POCKET MAP G4

Kadijksplein 5. cafekadijk.nl.

Tiny place which – contrary to what the homely interior with Delft blue crockery might suggest – has an excellent Indonesian inspired menu which is good for vegetarians and vegans. Start, perhaps, with the chicken or beef *saté* and for dessert try the traditional Indonesian *spekkoek* (spiced cake) served with coffee. €

Noorderlicht café

MAP PAGE 82, POCKET MAP E1

NDSM-Plein 102. noorderlichtcafe.nl.

Like a large greenhouse, the *Noorderlicht Café* is one of the grooviest café-restaurants on NDSM and has unusual origins: a group of squatters combined to build the place from recycled materials and, as a logical extension, opted to serve sustainably sourced food as well. It's a great spot to eat too, with a lively, international menu – try, for example, the Persian cauliflower omelette with almonds and fig tapenade. *Noorderlicht Café* is at its busiest on sunny summer weekends, when it also offers a programme of live music - and the crowd spills out over its grounds. €

Restaurants

A Tavola

MAP PAGE 80, POCKET MAP G4

Kadijksplein 9. atavolarestaurant.nl.

On a pleasant canalside square, this attractive restaurant serves up simple but delicious Italian food, including a first-rate selection of antipasti, pasta, meat and fish. Much of the produce comes from their own farm in Italy. €€€

Bimhuis

éénvistwéévis

MAP PAGE 80, POCKET MAP G4
Schippersgracht 6. Ⓦ eenvistweevis.nl.
A small and cosy fish restaurant serving an imaginative selection of seafood, such as seabass with rosemary and thyme and halibut with corn, onion and coriander. The fish is complemented by well-chosen wines – and the surroundings are suitably modish. €€

Gebroeders Hartering

MAP PAGE 80, POCKET MAP F4
Peperstraat 10. Ⓦ gebr-hartering.nl.
Run by two brothers, *Gebroeders Hartering* is a special occasion sort of place serving modern Dutch/European cuisine. Choose one of their set menus, from five and up to seven courses. Menus are always seasonal and often adventurous, with offal frequently appearing. If that sounds too wallet-searing, they do a la carte most of the time. Reservations essential. €€€€

Greetje

MAP PAGE 80, POCKET MAP F4
Peperstraat 23. Ⓦ restaurantgreetje.nl.
A cosy, busy restaurant that serves up Dutch staples with a modern twist. A changing menu reflects the seasons and the favourite dishes of the owner's mother – a native of southern Netherlands. Superb home-cooking in a great atmosphere. €€€

IJ-Kantine

MAP PAGE 82, POCKET MAP E1
NDSM Kade 5. Ⓦ ijkantine.nl.
Large, canteen-like restaurant and bar in a one-time industrial building a few paces from the ferry dock. Serves up a please-all menu of burgers, pasta and the like to a lively, youthful crew. €€

Pllek

MAP PAGE 82, POCKET MAP E1
T.T. Neveritaweg 59. Ⓦ pllek.nl.
One of several hipster places to have sprung up at the NDSM wharf, *Pllek* is arguably the best, its industrial vibe very appealing and oh so cool. Dishes are inventive, international and reasonably priced. DJs on Friday and Saturday nights. €€

Bars

De Druif

MAP PAGE 80, POCKET MAP G4
Rapenburgerplein 83.
"The Grape" is one of the city's oldest bars (dating from 1631), and certainly one of its more beguiling, the creaking timbers of its interior holding a platoon of old gin-dispensing barrels. A popular neighbourhood joint, it pulls in an easy-going crowd.

Hiding in Plain Sight

MAP PAGE 80, POCKET MAP F4
Rapenburg 18. Ⓦ hpsamsterdam.com.

Perhaps the best cocktail bar in Amsterdam, *Hiding in Plain Sight* is decorated in the style of an American speakeasy – or at least an approximation of it. The cocktail menu details what goes in where and what you can expect it to taste like, but although the menu changes frequently, it always includes a large selection of Mezcal-based drinks.

Clubs and live music

Bimhuis

MAP PAGE 80, POCKET MAP G2
Piet Heinkade 3. Ⓦ bimhuis.nl.
The city's premier jazz and improvised music venue is located right next to the Muziekgebouw, beside the River IJ. The *Bimhuis* showcases gigs from Dutch and international artists throughout the week, as well as jam sessions and workshops. There's also a bar and restaurant with pleasant views over the river.

Muziekgebouw aan 't ij

MAP PAGE 80, POCKET MAP G2
Piet Heinkade 1. Ⓦ muziekgebouw.nl.
Located in a striking modern glass building overlooking the river, the *Muziekgebouw* showcases everything from classical through to jazz and rock, and has studios, rehearsal space and convention facilities.

Panama

MAP PAGE 80, POCKET MAP H2
Oostelijke Handelskade 4. Ⓦ panama.nl.
All-in-one restaurant, bar and nightclub located in a former power plant perched right on the river IJ. Many live performances as well as internationally renowned DJs on weekends. One of the coolest spots in the city, *Panama* has played a leading role in spicing up the Eastern docklands.

THT/Paradiso Noord

MAP PAGE 82, POCKET MAP F1
IJpromenade 2. Ⓦ tolhuistuin.nl.
Metres from the EYE Film Institute, on the north bank of the River IJ, the Tolhuistuin is a somewhat dishevelled modern building, whose large interior is used for all manner of events and festivals as well as club nights under the banner 'Paradiso Noord'. See website for schedule.

Panama

The Museum Quarter and around

During the nineteenth century, Amsterdam grew beyond its restraining canals, gobbling up the surrounding countryside with a slew of new, mostly residential suburbs. One result was the creation of Museumplein, a large triangular open space surrounded by the cream of the city's museums. The largest is the Rijksmuseum, which occupies a huge late nineteenth-century edifice overlooking the Singelgracht and possessing an exceptional collection of art and applied art. Close by, the more modern Van Gogh Museum boasts the finest assortment of Van Gogh paintings in the world, while the adjacent Stedelijk Museum has an outstanding collection of modern art. Out on this side of the city also is the Vondelpark, Amsterdam's largest and most attractive green space, whose gently landscaped rectangle of lawns and paths, lakes and streams provides the perfect place for a lazy picnic between museums. The leafy streets around the park, such as P.C. Hooftstraat, also provide some of the most upmarket shopping in Amsterdam.

Museumplein

MAP PAGE 90, POCKET MAP C7

Extending south from Stadhouderskade to Van Baerlestraat, **Museumplein**'s wide lawns and gravelled spaces are used for a variety of outdoor activities, from visiting circuses to political demonstrations. There's a **war memorial** here too – it's the group of slim steel blocks about three-quarters of the way down the Museumplein on the left-hand side. It commemorates the women and children of the wartime concentration camps, particularly those who died at Ravensbruck.

Rijksmuseum

MAP PAGE 90, POCKET MAP C6

Museumstraat 1. Ⓦ rijksmuseum.nl. Charge.

The **Rijksmuseum** is without question the country's foremost museum, with one of the world's most comprehensive collections of seventeenth-century Dutch paintings, including twenty or so works by **Rembrandt** (1606–1669), plus a healthy sample of canvases by his contemporaries. These paintings, from Amsterdam's seventeenth-century 'Golden Age', are the museum's main pull, but the Rijksmuseum also owns an extravagant collection of paintings from every other pre-twentieth-century period of Dutch art as well as a vast hoard of applied art and sculpture. All are now shown to best advantage, following the 2013 completion of a thoroughgoing **refurbishment** that cost millions of euros. Bear in mind, though, that queues can be long, especially in summer and at weekends, so try to book online ahead of time, or come early in the morning.

Rijksmuseum's atrium

Above all, it's the seventeenth-century paintings that catch the eye. There are paintings by Rembrandt's pupils – Ferdinand Bol, Gerard Dou and Gabriel Metsu; several wonderful canvases by Frans Hals, such as his scatological *Merry Drinker*; the cool interiors of Gerard ter Borch and Pieter de Hooch; soft, tonal river scenes by the Haarlem artist Salomon van Ruysdael and Albert Cuyp; the urbane church interiors of Pieter Saenredam; the popular carousing peasants of Jan Steen; and the dreamy realism of Vermeer, as exemplified by the exquisite, lost-in-thought *Milkmaid* of 1660. However, it's the **Rembrandts** that steal the show, especially *The Night Watch* of 1642 – perhaps the most famous and probably the most valuable of all the artist's pictures – plus other key works, such as a late *Self-Portrait*, a touching depiction of his cowled son, *Titus*, the arresting *Staalmeesters* and *The Jewish Bride*, one of his very last pictures, finished in 1667.

Moco Museum

MAP PAGE 90, POCKET MAP B7
Honthorststraat 20. Ⓦ mocomuseum.com. Charge.

The Museum Quarter has burnished its artistic credentials with the opening of the **Moco Museum** of modern and contemporary art. Occupying a substantial, early twentieth-century brick building close to the Van Gogh Museum, the Moco concentrates on temporary, digital and immersive exhibitions, which have featured the likes of Banksy, Warhol and Yayoi Kusama.

Van Gogh Museum

MAP PAGE 90, POCKET MAP B7
Museumplein 6. Ⓦ vangoghmuseum.nl. Charge. Admission by timed ticket only; book online.

The **Van Gogh Museum**, comprising a world-beating collection of the work of **Vincent van Gogh** (1853–90), is one of Amsterdam's top attractions. The museum occupies two buildings, with the museum entrance to the

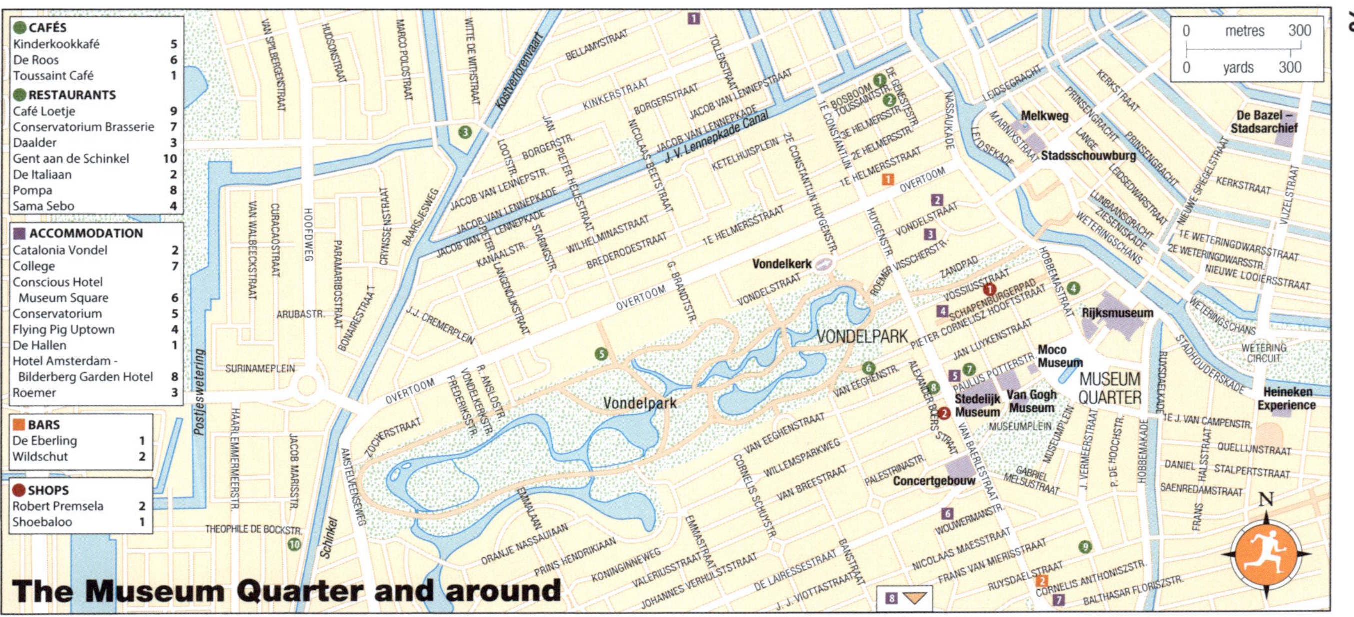
The Museum Quarter and around
CAFÉS
Kinderkookkafé 5
De Roos 6
Toussaint Café 1
RESTAURANTS
Café Loetje 9
Conservatorium Brasserie 7
Daalder 3
Gent aan de Schinkel 10
De Italiaan 2
Pompa 8
Sama Sebo 4
ACCOMMODATION
Catalonia Vondel 2
College 7
Conscious Hotel Museum Square 6
Conservatorium 5
Flying Pig Uptown 4
De Hallen 1
Hotel Amsterdam - Bilderberg Garden Hotel 8
Roemer 3
BARS
De Eberling 1
Wildschut 2
SHOPS
Robert Premsela 2
Shoebaloo 1
0 metres 300
0 yards 300
N
Vondelpark
VONDELPARK
MUSEUM QUARTER
Vondelkerk
Rijksmuseum
Moco Museum
Van Gogh Museum
Stedelijk Museum
Concertgebouw
Melkweg
Stadsschouwburg
De Bazel – Stadsarchief
Heineken Experience
J. V. Lennepkade Canal
Kostverlorenvaart
Schinkel
Postjeswetering
OVERTOOM
MUSEUMPLEIN
WETERING CIRCUIT

The Stedelijk Museum

rear via the ultramodern curved annexe, which was financed by a Japanese insurancc company – the same conglomerate that paid $35 million for one of van Gogh's *Sunflowers* canvases in 1987 – and provides temporary exhibition space. A ground- floor escalator connects the annexe with the main museum building, an angular structure designed by a leading light of the De Stijl movement, Gerrit Rietveld, and opened to the public in 1973. Beautifully presented and recently renovated, this part of the museum provides an introduction to the man and his art based on paintings that were mostly inherited from Vincent's art-dealer brother Theo. There are usually small supporting displays here too, mostly putting van Gogh into artistic context with the work of his friends and contemporaries: the museum owns paintings by the likes of Toulouse-Lautrec, Cézanne, Bernard, Seurat, Gauguin, Anton Mauve, Charles Daubigny, Pissarro and Monet.

All of van Gogh's key paintings are featured in the Rietveld building, displayed chronologically, starting with the dark, sombre works of the early years such as *The Potato Eaters* and finishing up with the asylum years at St Rémy and the final, tortured paintings done at Auvers, where van Gogh lodged for the last three months of his life, before his suicide. It was at Auvers that van Gogh painted the frantic *Wheatfield with Crows* and the disturbing *Tree Roots*.

The Stedelijk Museum

MAP PAGE 90, POCKET MAP B7

Museumplein 10. ⓦ stedelijk.nl. Charge.

The **Stedelijk Museum** has long been Amsterdam's number one venue for modern and contemporary art and design, and finally, after moving hither and thither, it returned to its original home on Museumplein in 2012 – but its

The Concertgebouw at night

original home with a difference: the nineteenth-century building has been entirely refurbished and attached to it now is a cumbersome new extension, derisively nicknamed "the bath tub". Inside, the museum focuses on cutting-edge, **temporary exhibitions** of modern art, from photography and video through to sculpture and collage, and these are supplemented by a regularly rotated selection from the museum's large and wide-ranging **permanent collection**. Among many highlights from this permanent collection is a particularly large sample of the work of **Piet Mondriaan** (1872–1944), from his early, muddy abstracts to the boldly coloured rectangular blocks for which he's most famous. The Stedelijk is also strong on **Kasimir Malevich** (1878–1935), whose dense attempts at Cubism lead to the dynamism and bold, primary tones of his "Suprematist" paintings – slices, blocks and bolts of colour that shift around as if about to resolve themselves into some complex computer graphic. Other high spots include several **Marc Chagall** (1887–1985) paintings and a number of works by American Abstract Expressionists Mark Rothko, Ellsworth Kelly and Barnett Newman, plus the odd piece by Lichtenstein, Warhol, Robert Ryman, Kooning and Jean Dubuffet.

Concertgebouw

MAP PAGE 90, POCKET MAP B7
Concertgebouwplein 10.
concertgebouw.nl.

The **Concertgebouw** (Concert Hall) is the home of the famed – and much recorded – Koninklijk (Royal) Concertgebouw Orchestra. When the German composer Brahms visited Amsterdam in the 1870s he was scathing about the locals' lack of culture and in particular their lack of an even halfway suitable venue for his music. In the face of such ridicule, a consortium of Amsterdam businessmen got together to fund the construction of a brand-new concert hall and the result was the Concertgebouw, completed in 1888. Since then, it has become renowned among musicians and concertgoers for its marvellous acoustics, and after a facelift and the replacement of its crumbling foundations in the early 1990s, it is looking and sounding better than ever. The acoustics of the Grote Zaal (Large Hall) are unparalleled, and the smaller Kleine Zaal regularly hosts chamber concerts. Prices vary enormously depending on who is appearing as well as the type of seat; tickets start at around €25.

Vondelpark

MAP PAGE 90, POCKET MAP A7

Multiple entrances, but main entrance on Stadshouderkade near its junction with Hobbemastraat. Ⓦ hetvondelpark.net. Free.

Amsterdam is short of green spaces, which makes the leafy expanses of the **Vondelpark**, a short stretch from Museumplein, doubly welcome. This is easily the largest and most popular of the city's parks, its network of footpaths used by a healthy slice of the city's population. The park dates back to 1864, when a group of leading Amsterdammers clubbed together to transform the soggy marshland that lay beyond the Leidsepoort into a landscaped park. The park possesses over one hundred species of tree, a wide variety of local and imported plants, and – among many incidental features – a bandstand, an excellent rose garden and a network of ponds and narrow waterways that are home to many sorts of wildfowl. There are other animals too: cows, sheep, hundreds of squirrels, plus a large colony of bright-green (and very noisy) parakeets. During the summer, the park regularly hosts free concerts and theatrical performances, mostly in its own specially designed open-air theatre. The park is named after Amsterdam's foremost poet, **Joost van den Vondel** (1587–1679), who ran a hosiery business here in the city, in between writing and hobnobbing with the local elite. Vondel was a kind of Dutch Shakespeare and his *Gijsbrecht van Amstel*, in which he celebrates Dutch life during the Golden Age, is one of the classics of Dutch literature. There's a large and somewhat grandiose statue of the man on a plinth near the main entrance to the park.

Vondelpark in autumn

Shops

Robert Premsela

MAP PAGE 90, POCKET MAP B7
Van Baerlestraat 78. ⊕ 020 662 4266.
This long-established bookshop has a number of specialisms, including architecture and photography, though art in general – and Dutch art in particular – comes top of the bibliographic pile. As you might expect, most books are in Dutch, but there is a good range of English titles as well.

Shoebaloo

MAP PAGE 90, POCKET MAP B6
P. C. Hooftstraat 80. ⓦ shoebaloo.nl.
The city's coolest shoe shop - on the city's slickest shopping street – catering for both men and women, with a mesmerizing, space-like interior. They also sell designer accessories. One of three Amsterdam outlets.

Cafés

Kinderkookkafé

MAP PAGE 90, POCKET MAP A6
Vondelpark 6b (Overtoom 325).
ⓦ kinderkookkafe.nl.
A café run by children aged 5–12, who cook, wait and wash dishes. Though this may sound like a recipe for disaster, the food – pizzas, sandwiches, cakes – is simple and (usually) tasty, and it's all good fun. Advance booking strongly recommended. €

De Roos

MAP PAGE 90, POCKET MAP B7
PC Hooftstraat 183. ⓦ roos.nl.
The downstairs café at this New Age centre on the edge of the Vondelpark is one of the most peaceful spots in the city, selling a range of drinks and organic snacks and meals. There's also a bookshop, plus yoga and meditation. €

Toussaint Café

MAP PAGE 90, POCKET MAP B5
Bosboom Toussaintstraat 26.
ⓦ cafe-toussaint.nl.
This cosy, neighbourhood café, not far from the Vondelpark, makes a nice spot for lunch – excellent sandwiches, waffles, toasties, *uitsmijters* and, for something a little different, tasty tapas too. €

Restaurants

Café Loetje

MAP PAGE 90, POCKET MAP C8
Johannes Vermeerstraat 52. ⓦ loetje.nl.
Excellent steaks, fries and salads are the order of the day here at this lively *eetcafé* and prices are very reasonable. The expansive outdoor terrace is a bonus in the summer time. €€

Conservatorium Brasserie

MAP PAGE 90, POCKET MAP B7
Paulus Potterstraat 50.
ⓦ conservatoriumhotel.com.
Inside the handsomely renovated *Conservatorium Hotel*, this chic and smart brasserie serves an all-day menu including salads and light bites – try, for example, the excellent caprese salad or the angus beef hamburger. Great glass-roofed courtyard venue. €€

Daalder

MAP PAGE 90, POCKET MAP A5
Postjesweg 1. ⓦ daalderamsterdam.nl.
Slick and sleek, top-ranking restaurant where the super-cool décor – think graphic shapes and street art – is a suitable setting for the Modern European haute cuisine – ravioli with beetroot and so forth. Lunch times are more affordable than the evenings. Reservations well-nigh essential. €€€€

Gent aan de Schinkel

MAP PAGE 90, POCKET MAP A6
Theophile de Bockstraat 1.
ⓦ gentaandeschinkel.nl.
Situated just outside the west end of the Vondelpark, across

Conservatorium Brasserie

the pedestrian bridge, this is an appealing corner restaurant on a busy canal, serving Belgian and fusion cuisine and a huge range of bottled Belgian beers to enjoy on their summer terrace. €€

De Italiaan

MAP PAGE 90, POCKET MAP B5
Bosboom Toussaintstraat 29.
Ⓦ deitaliaan.com.
Dull name and fairly spartan décor but the food is first-rate – Italian dishes, both a la carte and in a set menu, including the likes of sliced beef *tagliatella*. Also does an excellent range of pizzas cooked in a wood oven. €€

Pompa

MAP PAGE 90, POCKET MAP B7
Willemsparkweg 6.
Ⓦ pompa-restaurant.nl.
In the day time, this bright, modern café serves a good line in tapas, but in the evenings it morphs into an Italian-accented restaurant offering everything from classic *pasta vongole* to steak with truffle pesto. €€

Sama Sebo

MAP PAGE 90, POCKET MAP C6
P.C. Hooftstraat 27. Ⓦ samasebo.nl.
One of Amsterdam's prime Indonesian restaurants, much lauded for its *rijsttafel*, though less expensive dishes are on offer. Prompt and efficient service, warm and traditional decor. €€

Bars

De Ebeling

MAP PAGE 90, POCKET MAP B6
Overtoom 52. Ⓦ de-ebeling.nl.
Converted from an old bank (the toilets are in the vaults), this smart and chic lounge bar offers an inviting range of cocktails and beers on tap: try, for example, a 'Whiskey Sour' or a 'Moscow Mule'. Has a modern, comfortable vibe.

Wildschut

MAP PAGE 90, POCKET MAP C8
Roelof Hartplein 1. Ⓦ cafewildschut.nl.
Not far from the Concertgebouw, this bar is famous for its Art Deco furnishings and fittings as well as its large and popular pavement patio. The nicest place to drink in the area, plus an extensive bar menu – everything from salads and sandwiches through to burgers and chicken spring rolls.

De Pijp, Nieuw Zuid and Amsterdam Oost

Amsterdam is a small city, and the majority of its residential outer districts are easily reached from the city centre by tram. The south holds most of interest, kicking off with the vibrant De Pijp quarter, home to the Heineken Experience, and the 1930s architecture of the Nieuw Zuid (New South), which is also near the enjoyable woodland area of the Amsterdamse Bos. As for the other outer districts, you'll find a good deal less reason to make the effort, although the Tropenmuseum, a short walk from the Muiderpoort gate in Amsterdam Oost (East), is worth a special journey.

De Pijp

MAP PAGE 96, POCKET MAP D7

Across the Singelgracht from the Wetering Circuit lies the busy heart of the Oud Zuid (Old South) – the district known as **De Pijp** ("The Pipe"), Amsterdam's first real suburb. New development beyond the Singelgracht began around 1870, but after laying down the street plans, the city council left the actual house-building to private developers. They

Interior of the Heineken Experience

made the most of the arrangement and constructed long rows of cheaply built and largely featureless three- and four-storey buildings, and it is these that still dominate the area today. The district's name comes from the characteristically narrow terraced streets running between long, sombre canyons of brick tenements: the apartments here were said to resemble pipe-drawers, since each had a tiny street frontage but extended deep into the building. De Pijp remains one of the city's more closely-knit communities, and is home to a large proportion of new arrivals – Surinamese, Moroccan, Turkish and Asian.

Tram #24, beginning at Centraal Station, travels along the northern part of De Pijp's main drag, Ferdinand Bolstraat, as far as Albert Cuypstraat.

The Wetering circuit

MAP PAGE 100, POCKET MAP D7

At the southern end of Vijzelgracht, on the way to De Pijp from the city centre, is the **Wetering circuit** roundabout, which has two low-key memorials to World War II. On the southwestern corner of the roundabout, by the canal, is a sculpture of a wounded man holding a bugle; it was here, on March 12, 1945, that thirty people were shot by the Germans in reprisal for acts of sabotage by the Dutch Resistance – given that the war was all but over, it's hard to imagine a crueller or more futile action. Across the roundabout, the second memorial, in the form of a brick wall, commemorates H.M. van Randwijk, a Resistance leader who survived capture and interrogation by the Germans.

Heineken Experience

MAP PAGE 96, POCKET MAP D7

Stadhouderskade 78.

heinekenexperience.com. Charge, with discount if booked online.

On the northern edge of De Pijp is the former **Heineken brewery**, a whopping modern building set beside the Singelgracht canal and now reconfigured as the **Heineken Experience**. The brewery was Heineken's headquarters from 1864 to 1988, when the company was restructured and brewing was moved to a location out of town. Since then, Heineken has developed the site as a tourist attraction with lots of gimmicky but fun attractions such as virtual reality tours and displays on the history of Heineken, from advertising campaigns to beer-making. The old brewing facilities with their vast copper vats are included on the tour, but for many the main draw is the free beer you get to quaff at the end in the bar.

Albert Cuypmarkt

MAP PAGE 96, POCKET MAP D7-E7

Ferdinand Bolstraat, running north–south, is De Pijp's main street, but the long east–west thoroughfare of **Albert Cuypstraat** is its heart. The general **market** here (daily except Sun 9am–5pm) – which stretches for over 1km between Ferdinand Bolstraat and Van Woustraat – is the largest in the city, with a huge array of stalls selling everything from raw-herring sandwiches to saucepans. Check out the international shops that flank the market on each side, and the good-value Indian and Surinamese restaurants down the side streets.

Sarphatipark

MAP PAGE 96, POCKET MAP E8

Tram #3 runs along the south side of the park, and tram #4 from Centraal Station travels along Van Woustraat, 1 block east – get off at Ceintuurbaan.

Sarphatipark provides a welcome splash of greenery among the surrounding brick and concrete. The park, complete with footpaths and a sinewy lake, was laid out before the construction of De Pijp got underway, and was initially intended as a place for the bourgeoisie to take a stroll, parading their parasols and bustles.

Nieuw Zuid

MAP PAGE 100, POCKET MAP B9

Southwest of De Pijp, the **Nieuw Zuid** (New South) was the first properly planned extension to the city since the concentric canals of the seventeenth century.

Freddy Heineken

Heineken may not be the finest lager in the world, but no other brewer, Guinness apart, has thought up such catchy advertising slogans: "Heineken refreshes the parts other beers cannot reach", for one, is well-nigh impossible to beat. Alfred ("Freddy") Heineken (1923–2002) was the mastermind behind the company's rise to alcoholic success, but his route was far from straightforward. The company was founded in 1864 by Alfred's grandfather, Gerard, but his son and successor, Henry Pierre, sold the family's majority stake in 1942. Freddy didn't like this at all, but over time he skillfully amassed a majority shareholding. Chairman from 1979, Freddy ran the company with a beady eye for the main chance, increasing its sales dramatically both at home and abroad, while simultaneously developing a reputation as a playboy, or, more euphemistically, "bon vivant". Whatever the term, Freddy was hardly subtle: allegedly, the bedroom suite at the back of his office had a four-poster bed and a painting of a naked woman stroking a cat entitled The Woman with Two Pussies. In 1983 Freddy was kidnapped by three masked men and held for three weeks, before the police finally rescued him. Thereafter, he withdrew from the public eye, but maintained close relations with many of the country's richest and most powerful citizens until his death.

Albert Cuypmarkt

The Dutch architect Hendrik Petrus Berlage (1856–1934) was responsible for the overall plan, but much of the implementation passed to a pair of prominent architects of the Amsterdam School, Michael de Klerk and Piet Kramer, and it's the playful vision of these two – turrets and bulging windows, sloping roofs and frilly balustrades – that you see in some of the buildings of the Nieuw Zuid today. These architectural peccadilloes have helped make the Nieuw Zuid one of Amsterdam's most sought-after addresses. The prime example of the area's original style is **De Dageraad,** the housing estate located just north of the Amstel canal, while long, wide and leafy **Apollolaan** is home to some of the city's most attractive – and expensive – properties. The district's scenic high point is the languid greenery of the **Beatrixpark**, whose well-tended lawns and copses are intercepted by a gentle weave of canals.

The Amsterdam Hilton

MAP PAGE 100, POCKET MAP A9
Apollolaan 138.

One historic footnote that might entice you this far south is the **Amsterdam Hilton**, a standard-issue 1960s mini-tower block, where John Lennon and Yoko Ono staged their famous, week-long "Bed-In" for peace in 1969; you can still stay in the room where it all happened – the "John & Yoko Suite". More recently the *Hilton* was the centre of Dutch media attention when in 2010, Herman Brood – a Dutch singer, painter and addict – took his own life by jumping from the roof.

De Dageraad

MAP PAGE 96, POCKET MAP E9
Beginning at Centraal Station, Tram #4 runs along Van Woustraat; get off at Jozef Israelskade – the Amstelkade stop – and it's a 5min walk to De Dageraad.

Built between 1919 and 1922, the **De Dageraad** housing project was – indeed, is – public housing inspired by socialist utopianism, a grand vision built to elevate the working class, hence its name, "The Dawn". The handsome brick and stone work of the Berlage Lyceum marks the start of De Dageraad, with 350 workers' houses stretching beyond to either side of Pieter Lodewijk Takstraat and Burgemeester Tellegenstraat. The architects used a reinforced concrete frame as an underlay to each house, thus permitting folds, tucks and curves in the brick exteriors. Strong, angular doors, sloping roofs and turrets punctuate the facades, and you'll find a corner tower at the end of every block – it's stunning.

Amsterdamse Bos

MAP PAGE 100, POCKET MAP B9
Main entrance at the junction of Amstelveenseweg and Van Nijenrodeweg, 3km south of the west end of the Vondelpark. Various transport options including tram #24 from Centraal Station to the Vu Medisch Centrum stop and a 15min-walk. ⓦ amsterdamsebos.nl.

With ten square kilometres of wooded parkland, the **Amsterdamse Bos** (Amsterdam Forest), to the southwest of the Nieuw Zuid, is the city's largest open space. Planted during the 1930s, the park was a large-scale attempt to provide gainful work for the city's unemployed. Originally a bleak area of flat and marshy fields, it combines a rural feel with that of a well-tended city park – and thus the "forest" tag is something of a misnomer.

In the north of the Bos, the main entrance leads to the **Bezoekerscentrum** at Bosbaanweg 5 (visitor centre; Tues–Sun 10am–5pm; free; ⓣ 020 251 7840), where you can pick up maps and information. Behind the centre is the **Bosbaan**, a kilometre-long dead-straight canal, popular for boating and swimming, and there are children's playgrounds and spaces for various sports, including ice skating. Canoes and rowing boats can be rented just to the south of the Bosbaan, beside the Grote Vijver Lake at **Kanoverhuur**

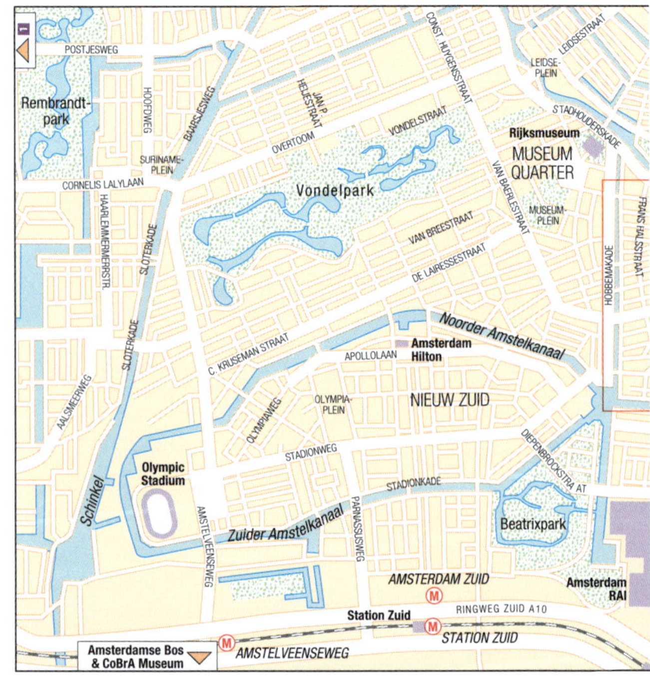

Amsterdamse Bos (April–Sept daily 10.30am–6pm; ⓣ 020 645 7831, ⓦ kanoverhuur-adam.nl), or you can simply walk or jog your way around a choice of clearly marked trails. There's bicycle rental here too, beside the main entrance at Amsterdamse Bos Fietsverhuur (daily 10am–6pm; ⓣ 020 644 5473, ⓦ amsterdamsebosfietsverhuur.nl). Possibly one of the best ways to explore the winding trails of the parkland.

CoBrA Museum

MAP PAGE 100, POCKET MAP B9
Sandbergplein 1, Amstelveen. ⓦ cobra-museum.nl. Charge.

The **CoBrA Museum of Modern Art**, located well to the south of the Amsterdamse Bos, has an attractive setting, its glass walls giving a view of the canal behind. The museum features the works of the artists of the CoBrA movement, which was founded in 1948. The movement grew out of artistic developments in the cities of Copenhagen, Brussels and Amsterdam – hence the name (a curled snake later became the symbol of the movement). CoBrA's first exhibition, held at Amsterdam's Stedelijk Museum, showcased the big, colourful canvases, with bold lines and confident forms, for which the movement became famous. The work displayed a spontaneity that was unusual for the art world of the time and it stirred a veritable hornet's nest of artistic controversy. You'll only find a scattering of the paintings in the gallery, but there's enough to get an idea of what CoBrA was about, not least in **Karel Appel**'s (1921–2006) weird bird sculpture outside, and his brash, childlike paintings inside. Appel, along with **Constant Nieuwenhuys**, was one of the movement's leading

lights. Upstairs, the museum hosts regular temporary exhibitions of works by contemporary artists. There's a good shop, too, with plenty of prints and books on CoBrA, plus a bright café serving up tasty and inventive lunch options where you can gaze upon Appel's sculpture at length.

The Muiderpoort

MAP PAGE 100, POCKET MAP H6
South end of Plantage Middenlaan.

Amsterdam Oost begins with Amsterdam's old eastern gate, the **Muiderpoort**, a grand and domineering Neoclassical affair through which Napoleon staged a triumphal entry into the city in 1811. The grandness of the occasion was, however, tempered by his half-starved troops, who could barely be restrained from looting a city which was to them brimming with potential spoils.

Display at the Tropenmuseum

Tropenmuseum

MAP PAGE 100, POCKET MAP H6
Linnaeusstraat 2. Tram #14 from Centraal Station to Alexanderplein. ⓦ tropenmuseum.nl. Charge.

Amsterdam East's main attraction is the **Tropenmuseum**, which occupies a rambling brick building beside the Singelgracht canal. Part of the **Royal Tropical Institute**, this large ethnographic museum has room to focus on themes such as the world's cultural and historical influences, and impresses with its applied art.

One particularly interesting section is dedicated to **Dutch colonialism**, focusing on Indonesia and the Pacific. Among the many artefacts, there are Javanese stone friezes, elaborate carved wooden boats from New Guinea and, perhaps strangest of all, ritual ancestor "Bis poles" cut from giant New Guinea mangroves. The collection is imaginatively presented and there are also creative and engaging displays devoted to such subjects as music-making and puppetry. In addition, there are intriguing and largely successful reconstructions, down to sounds and smells, of typical settings from different countries, such as a Jamaican café or a Surinamese logger's hut.

Oosterpark

MAP PAGE 100, POCKET MAP H6-7
Tram #14 from Centraal Station to Alexanderplein & a 5min-walk.

Next to the Tropenmuseum, the **Oosterpark** is a large slab of greenery whose mature trees, footpaths and bandstand flank a wiggly lake. It's a popular picnic spot and, while you're here, you can hunt out a couple of interesting **monuments**: the more recent is *De Schreeuw* (*The Cry*), dedicated to the film-maker Theo van Gogh, who was murdered in Amsterdam in 2004; the other is the National Slavery Monument, erected in 2002 to commemorate the (rather reluctant) abolition of slavery in the Netherlands in 1863.

Green House on Voorburgwal

Shops

Beadazzled

MAP PAGE 96, POCKET MAP D8
Sarphatipark 6. beadazzled.nl.
Beads in all shapes and colours as well as bags, cheerfully decorated lamps and other accessories, including Havaiana flip-flops for men, women and children. Two specialities are their Japanese *miyuki* seed beads and *katsuki* beads.

Blond

MAP PAGE 96, POCKET MAP D7
Ferdinand Bolstraat 44. blond-amsterdam.com.
Popular gift shop with hand-painted and personalized pottery, bed linen, towels and note blocks, mainly in the colour pink. There's a nice café too.

Coffeeshops

Greenhouse

MAP PAGE 100, POCKET MAP F8
Tolstraat 91. greenhousecoffeeshops.com.
Consistently sweeps the boards at the annual Cannabis Cup, with medals for its dope as well as "Best Coffeeshop" – these guys are extremely knowledgeable in their field. Tolstraat is down to the south of De Pijp, but worth the trek: if you're only buying once, buy here. Also a branch nearer the centre at O.Z. Voorburgwal 191.

Katsu Coffeeshop

MAP PAGE 96, POCKET MAP D8
Eerste van der Helststraat 70. katsu.nl
Welcoming and relaxing spot with hippy vibes. Please note the breathing grassy knoll in the back room is animated and not actually breathing…

Cafés

Factory Girl

MAP PAGE 96, POCKET MAP D7
Saenredamstraat 32. factorygirl.net.
A hip spot for brunch or lunch with a focus on healthy vegetarian food that makes you feel good. There's a whole host of creative breakfast options (think potatoes and eggs Catalan style or Turkish eggs with plant-based yoghurt sauce and an herb-infused vegan butter). They also

Teppanyaki Sazanka, Hotel Okura

have a great range of vegan baked goods – don't leave without a vegan cinnamon bun. €

Vishandel Molenaar

MAP PAGE 96, POCKET MAP D7
Albert Cuypstraat 93. ⓣ 020 673 5955.
What better way to round off your visit to the Albert Cuypstraat market than to sample the delights of this excellent – and typical – Dutch fish stall. If you're not brave enough for the raw herring there are cooked offerings too, even calamari. €

Restaurants

De Duvel

MAP PAGE 96, POCKET MAP D8
1e van der Helststraat 59–61. ⓦ deduvel.nl.
Immensely popular, boho-style *eetcafé*, always crowded, so be sure to book ahead. Toasties and sandwiches at lunchtimes; mains such as steaks, *saté* and spaghetti at dinner. Also a popular drinking spot, especially on a warm and sunny evening when the outside pavement terrace is a fine place to be. €

Hotel Okura

MAP PAGE 96, POCKET MAP D9
Ferdinand Bolstraat 333. ⓦ okura.nl.
The chi-chi *Hotel Okura* has four restaurants, no fewer than three of which have/had Michelin stars: the *Yamazato* is the finest experience of Japanese food you'll find in the city, a traditional kaiseki restaurant whose menu features expertly prepared sushi, tempura, sashimi and sukiyaki. Alternatively, try the *Teppanyaki Sazanka*, a much vaunted grill restaurant, where the chef prepares fish, steaks and vegetables on a hot plate in front of you. In both cases, booking essential. €€€€

Little Collins

MAP PAGE 96, POCKET MAP E7
1e Sweelinkckstraat 19F. ⓦ littlecollins.nl.
A little piece of Australia in Amsterdam, serving more or less anything you like – oysters, pork rillettes, Korean beef, pork belly and more. Be prepared to wait for a table. €

Spaghetteria

MAP PAGE 100, POCKET MAP F8
Van Woustraat 123. ⓦ spaghetteria.com.
Informal and fast-moving pasta bar with long, communal wooden tables and a menu offering half a dozen pasta dishes that change daily. One particular recommendation is the tagliatelle with mussels, clams, cherry tomatoes and parsley in white wine. One of a ten-place chain. €

De Waaghals

MAP PAGE 96, POCKET MAP D7
Frans Halsstraat 29. ⓦ waaghals.nl.
Well-prepared organic dishes in this cooperative-run veggie restaurant a short stroll north of Albert Cuypstraat. This place gets busy early so book ahead to be sure of a table. The menu changes twice a month, and though the food takes a while to prepare, the rewards are delicious and generously portioned. €

Warung Spang Makandra

MAP PAGE 96, POCKET MAP D8
Gerard Doustraat 39. ⓦ spangmakandra.nl.
Bargain-basement Surinamese-Javanese *eetcafé*, in business since 1978. Most dishes are under €13, and you can get delicious

Surinamese sandwiches for €4.50. Great flavours – and an excellent budget choice. Try, for example, the tasty and tangy chicken satay. €

Bars

Café Krull

MAP PAGE 96, POCKET MAP D8
Sarphatipark 2. 020 662 0214.
A few metres from the Albert Cuyp, this is an atmospheric and lively place though the décor is routine. Drinks all day long, a decent light lunch menu and good music.

De Groene Vlinder

MAP PAGE 96, POCKET MAP D8
Albert Cuypstraat 130.
cafe-de-groene-vlinder.nl.
Great views of the bustling market from this bright and spacious split-level café with inexpensive daily specials and bulky salads. The drinks menu covers all the basics and then some with at least six beers on tap.

Pilsvogel

MAP PAGE 96, POCKET MAP D7
Gerard Douplein 14. pilsvogel.nl.
Favourite drinking spot for style-conscious 30-somethings, who gather here to enjoy the laidback atmosphere and decent tapas, as well as a good selection of wine.

Wynbar Boelen & Boelen

MAP PAGE 96, POCKET MAP D7
1e van der Helststraat 50. wijnbar.nl.
Tasteful wine bar close to Albert Cuypstraat market with a huge selection of wines. A heated terrace provides alfresco eating even in the cooler months, and the French-inspired menu offers seafood delights such as a half-dozen oysters.

Club

Hotel Arena

MAP PAGE 100, POCKET MAP H6
's-Gravensandestraat 55. Metro from Centraal Station to Weesperplein & an 8min walk. hotelarena.nl.
Hip club set in a restored chapel adjoining a deluxe hotel that used to be an orphanage and an asylum. Open for parties and special events. International DJs sometimes drop by – and there's a great cocktail lounge here too.

Hotel Arena

Day-trips from Amsterdam

Amsterdammers may well tell you that there's nothing remotely worth seeing outside their own city, but the fact is you're spoilt for choice, with fast and efficient rail connections putting about a third of the country within easy reach of a day-trip. There are any number of places you can get to, including most of the towns of the Randstaad conurbation that stretches south and east of Amsterdam and encompasses the country's other big cities, The Hague, Utrecht and Rotterdam, but we've picked a few of the closer highlights. The easiest trip you could make is to Haarlem, just fifteen minutes away by train, a pleasant provincial town that is home to the outstanding Frans Hals Museum. There's also the showcase of the country's flower growers, the Keukenhof Gardens, worth visiting in spring and summer, while to the north of Amsterdam the most obvious targets are Volendam and Marken, two old seaports bordering the freshwater IJsselmeer and Markermeer lakes, formerly – before the enclosing dykes were put in – the saltwater Zuider Zee. No trains venture out along this part of the coast, but it's an easy bus ride from Amsterdam, also taking in the beguiling one-time shipbuilding centre of Edam, which is, of course, famous for its cheese. A little further afield – and this time on the train network – is the charming seaport of Enkhuizen.

Haarlem

An easy fifteen-minute train journey (6 hourly) from Amsterdam's Centraal Station, **Haarlem** has a very different feel from its big-city neighbour. Once a flourishing cloth-making centre, the town avoided the worst excesses of industrialization and nowadays it's an easily absorbed place with an attractive centre studded with fine old buildings. The best place to start an exploration is the **Grote Kerk** (W bavo.nl; Mon–Sat 10am–5pm; charge), a soaring Gothic church with a magnificent medieval nave which is located right in the centre of town on the Grote Markt. But the real draw is the outstanding **Frans Hals Museum**, whose principal gallery is located in the Oudemannhuis, or almshouse, a five-minute stroll south from the Grote Markt at Groot Heiligland 62 (Tues–Sat 11am–5pm, Sun noon–5pm; charge; T 023 511 5775, W franshalsmuseum.nl). Chief among the Hals' paintings is the set of "Civic Guard" group portraits with which he made his name. Displayed together, these make a powerful impression, but the artist's later, darker works, created when Hals lived here in the almshouse – and reminiscent of Rembrandt's later paintings – are

Keukenhof Gardens

his most brilliant and evocative. Most notable amongst them are the twin Regents and Regentesses of the Oudemannenhuis itself. The museum also boasts a hatful of works by Haarlem painters other than Hals, with canvases by Jan van Scorel, Karel van Mander and Cornelis Cornelisz van Haarlem.

Keukenhof Gardens

Stationsweg 166, Lisse. Ⓦ keukenhof.nl. Charge.

The pancake-flat fields extending south from Haarlem towards Leiden are the heart of the **Dutch bulbfields**, whose bulbs and blooms support a billion-dollar industry and some ten-thousand growers, as well as attracting tourists in droves. The small town of **Lisse**, halfway between Leiden and Haarlem, is home to the showcase **Keukenhof Gardens**, the largest flower gardens in the world. The site is the former estate of a fifteenth-century countess, who used to grow herbs and vegetables for her dining table, hence "Keukenhof", literally "kitchen garden". Some seven million flowers are on show for their full flowering period, complemented, in case of especially harsh winters, by 5000 square metres of glasshouses holding indoor displays. You could easily spend a whole day here, swooning among the sheer abundance of it all, but to get the best of it you need to come early, before the tour buses pack the place. There are several restaurants in the extensive grounds, and well-marked paths take you all the way through the gardens, which specialize in daffodils, hyacinths and, of course, tulips.

There are several ways to get to the Keukenhof by public transport from Amsterdam, but one of the simplest is to take the train from Amsterdam Centraal to Leiden Centraal (every 20min; 40min), then catch bus #50 from the neighbouring bus station; get off at Lisse, Vreewijk from where it's a 20min (1.4km) walk. Slightly more expensive, but a good deal quicker, is the Arriva Keukenhof Express bus #852 (Ⓦ arriva.nl), which runs direct from Amsterdam to the Keukenhof during the opening season.

Volendam

Edging the freshwater Markermeer, the former fishing village of **Volendam** was once something of an artists' retreat, visited by Renoir and Picasso and long a favoured location for local painters. The **Volendams Museum**, on the edge of the town centre at Zeestraat 41 (Ⓣ 029 936 9258, Ⓦ volendamsmuseum.nl; charge), tracks through the village's history and has lots of local artwork on display. It's also worth popping into the waterfront *Hotel Spaander*, where the public rooms are decorated with paintings and sketches given to the hotel by impoverished artists in lieu of rent.

Volendam is reachable from the bus station at the back of Amsterdam Centraal by EBS bus #316 (every 30min; 30min; Ⓦ localbus.nl); get off on Julianaweg, about 400m from the waterfront along Zeestraat. The bus also runs to Edam (10min), and although there are no buses from Volendam to Marken, there is a passenger ferry (March–Oct daily 10am–6pm, every 30min–1hr; Nov–Feb limited service; 25min; Ⓦ markenexpress.nl; charge either one way or return).

Marken

The tiny island of **Marken** was pretty much a closed community, supported by a small fishing industry, until its road connection to the mainland was completed in 1957. Nowadays, the fishing has all but disappeared, but the island – or rather its one and only village, Marken – retains a picturesque charm of immaculately maintained green wooden houses, clustered on top of mounds first raised to protect the islanders from the sea. There are two main parts to the village: waterfront **Havenbuurt**, which is dotted with

Marken

souvenir shops, often staffed by locals in traditional costume; and the quieter **Kerkbuurt**, centred on the church, whose narrow lanes are lined by ancient dwellings and one-time eel-smoking houses.

You can take a passenger ferry to Marken from Volendam; or you can get there direct from the Noord bus station at the end of Amsterdam's Metro Line #52 on EBS bus #315 (every 30min; 40min; Ⓦ localbus.nl). In Marken, passengers are dropped off beside the car park on the edge of the village, from where it's a five-minute walk to the waterfront. Note that there are currently no direct buses from Marken to Edam or Volendam.

Edam

Considering the international fame of the red balls of cheese that carry its name, you might expect the village of **Edam**, just 12km or so up along the coast from Marken, to be jam-packed with tourists. In fact, Edam usually lacks the crowds of its island neighbour and remains a delightful, good-looking and prosperous little town of neat brick houses and slender canals. Nowadays, the one real crowd puller is Edam's **cheese market**, held every Wednesday morning from July to mid-August on the Kaasmarkt (10.30am–12.30pm), but the real pleasure is in wandering its charming streets and canals, and maybe renting a bike to cycle down to the Markemeer lake. Bike rental is available at Ronald Schot, Grote Kerkstraat 9 (Ⓣ 029 937 2155, Ⓦ ronaldschot.nl). EBS bus #316 (every 30min; 40min; Ⓦ localbus.nl), links the bus station at the back of Amsterdam Centraal Station with Edam's bus station on the southwest edge of town, on Singelweg, a 5–10-minute walk from the centre. The bus also goes to Volendam, 3km away (10min). Note that there are no buses from Edam to Marken.

Enkhuizen

Nudging up against the waters of the IJsselmeer, **Enkhuizen** (trains from Amsterdam Centraal every 30min; 1hr) was once one of the country's most important seaports. Nowadays,

Enkhuizen

things are much quieter, but the town centre, with its ancient streets, slender canals and pretty harbours, is wonderfully well preserved, a rough circle with a ring of bastions and moat on one side, and the old sea dyke on the other. Strolling in from the train station, you soon reach the picturesque **Buitenhaven**, with its sailing boats and barges, and just beyond is the **Oude Haven**, which stretches east in a gentle curve to the conspicuous **Drommedaris**, a heavy-duty brick watchtower built in 1540 to guard the harbour entrance. Not far from the Drommedaris is the town's star turn, the excellent **Zuiderzeemuseum**, which divides into two, beginning with an indoor section on Wierdijk (daily 10am–5pm; charge; T 022 835 1111, W zuiderzeemuseum.nl), where around a dozen rooms are devoted to exhibitions on different aspects of the Zuider Zee. Nearby is the outdoor section, the Museumpark (April to late Oct daily 10am–5pm), which comprises a collection of original buildings moved here over the last decades. Highlights of the indoor section are concentrated in the impressive ship hall, where you can get up close and personal with a number of traditional sailing barges and other craft, for example a dinghy for duck-hunting, complete with shotgun. In the Museumpark, there are vintage stores, workshops and even streets that have been transported here from every part of the region, and which together provide the flavour of life hereabouts from 1880 to around 1932. Just about everything is worth seeing, but high points include a reconstruction of Marken harbour as of 1900, old fishermen's houses from Urk, a post office and a pharmacy that has a marvellous collection of "gapers" – painted wooden heads with their tongues out, which were the traditional sign of a pharmacist. The museum strives to be authentic: sheep and goats roam the surrounding meadows, its smokehouses smoke (and sell) herring and eels, and the sweetshop sells real old-fashioned sweets.

Bars

L'Auberge Damhotel

Keizersgracht 1, Edam. damhotel.nl.

This delightful boutique hotel, with its ornate vintage décor, has an infinitely cosy bar and pavement terrace, where you can get a tasty lunch of tapas, sandwiches and so forth – try, for example, the meatballs with tomato sauce or the beef with noodles. There's an upmarket restaurant here too – and, should you decide to stay the night, the hotel's eleven rooms are charming, each decorated in plush style – sweeping drapes and wide wooden bedheads. Accommodation €€€; bar food €€

De Jopenkerk

Gedempte Voldersgracht 2, Haarlem. jopenkerk.nl.

This converted old church is a microbrewery bar and restaurant rolled into one, with long benches, comfy sofas and its own cloudy, unfiltered beer. The food is simple and hearty rather than splendid, but you should at least try one of the dozen or so Jopen brews at the bar. €

Restaurants

Art Hotel Spaander

Haven 15–19, Volendam. spaander.com.

This creaky and atmospheric old hotel, perched right on the waterfront, is very much the hub of Volendam, with a nice bar for a drink or a coffee and a good brasserie serving lots of fishy specialities for lunch and dinner. The hotel's biggest pull is the paintings on the walls, nineteenth-century canvases for the most part, sometimes given in exchange for food and lodgings in a long-forgotten custom. €€

Drie Haringhe

Breedstraat 158, Enkhuizen. drieharinghebistro.nl.

Arguably Enkhuizen's finest restaurant, offering inventive, French-Mediterranean cuisine in smartly renovated cottage-like premises a block back from the harbour. Seafood is, as you might expect from the name ('The Three Herrings'), the speciality here, but there are also delights like the quail with apricots and sweet potato. €€€

Jacobus Pieck

Warmoesstraat 18, Haarlem. jacobuspieck.nl.

Welcoming, briskly decorated place that's a good bet for both lunch and dinner, with burgers and salads during the day and a slightly more ambitious menu in the evening – try, for instance, the salmon with couscous salad and chips. There's a secluded garden too. €

Land en Zeezicht

Havenbuurt 6, Marken. restaurantlezz.nl.

More of a lunch than dinner spot, but very cosy, overlooking the harbour and serving a mean smoked-eel sandwich. Quaint if somewhat staid décor, too, and very popular with day trippers. €

ML

Klokhuisplein 9, Haarlem. mlinhaarlem.nl.

Smart, slick and popular, this is Haarlem's best brasserie and restaurant, serving up mouth-watering fish and meat dishes prepared in innovative ways – try, for example, the grilled bass with tomato risotto and anchovies. As you might expect, the brasserie is a good wedge less expensive than the restaurant. €€€

Schipperscafé 'T Ankertje

Dijk 6. cafe-ankertje.nl.

Right beside the conspicuous Drommedaris, overlooking the inner harbour, this popular bar and restaurant has nautical knick-knacks hanging on the walls and a large waterside terrace. Filling food for a bargain price. €

ACCOMMODATION

The Dylan

Accommodation

Despite a slew of new hotels, from chic designer places through to chain high-rises, hotel accommodation in Amsterdam can still be difficult to find and is, more often than not, a major expense. Indeed, such is the city's popularity as a short-break destination that advance reservations are pretty much essential at any time of the year, though there tends to be more slack on Sunday and Monday nights. Prices fluctuate wildly with demand, so the rates we quote should serve only as a broad guideline. Prices are usually more affordable further from the centre – a standard-issue double room in the Grachtengordel can, for example, cost twice as much as a comparable room in the suburbs.

Hotels

The least expensive hotels charge around €150 for a double room, a little less if you share a bathroom, but don't expect too much in the way of creature comforts at these sort of prices – you only really hit any sort of comfort zone at about €220. Breakfast – bread, jam, eggs, ham and cheese – is usually included in the price of a room, but at budget and moderately priced hotels, it's often extra. One other thing to bear in mind: some of the cheaper hotels request full payment in advance or on arrival.

The Old Centre

THE EXCHANGE MAP PAGE 26, POCKET MAP B11. **Damrak 50. ⓦ hoteltheexchange.com.** Heaven knows, Damrak needs a decent hotel, and this sister to the excellent *Lloyd Hotel* is a welcome and wacky addition, with the same range of budget to luxury rooms, each eccentrically designed by students of the Amsterdam Fashion Institute. Full of cool character, and for the price one of the best places to sleep in town. There's also a sleek downstairs café, *Stock*. €€€

Accommodation price codes

All the **accommodation** detailed in this Guide has been graded according to the four price categories listed below. These represent how much you can expect to pay in each establishment for the **least expensive double or twin room with breakfast in high season** barring special deals and discounts; for a single room, expect to pay around eighty percent of the price of a double. Our categories are simply a guide to prices and do not give an indication of the facilities you might expect; as such they differ from the star-system applied by the tourist authorities.

€ = €50–100
€€ = €101–150
€€€ = €151–220
€€€€ = €221+

GRAND HOTEL AMRÂTH MAP PAGE 26, POCKET MAP D11. **Prins Hendrikkade 108.** ⓦ **amrathamsterdam.com.** Immaculate, five-star hotel occupying one of the city's most extraordinary buildings, an Expressionist confection that was once the HQ of a major shipping line. Perhaps inevitably, the rooms don't quite live up to their setting – but they are attractively appointed with all mod cons. €€€€

HOTEL DE L'EUROPE MAP PAGE 26, POCKET MAP B14. **Nieuwe Doelenstraat 2–14.** ⓦ **deleurope.com.** One of the city's top hotels, and retaining a wonderful fin-de-siècle charm, with large, well-furnished rooms, an attractive riverside terrace and a great central location. A canal view will cost you another €50 or so, but this is about as luxurious as the city gets. €€€€

LE COIN MAP PAGE 26, POCKET MAP B14. **Nieuwe Doelenstraat 5.** ⓦ **lecoin.nl.** In a good location opposite the swanky *Hotel de l'Europe*, but a quarter of the price. All rooms have kitchenettes and are kitted out in efficient modern style. Breakfast not included. €€€

MISC MAP PAGE 26, POCKET MAP C12. **Kloveniersburgwal 20.** ⓦ **misceatdrinksleep.com.** Excellent, very friendly independent hotel on the edge of the Red Light District, with six good-sized rooms each with a different theme and with some nice, stylish touches. Breakfast included. €€€

NH CITY CENTRE MAP PAGE 26, POCKET MAP A13. **Spuistraat 288.** ⓦ **nh-hotels.com.** A chain hotel, but an appealing one, in a sympathetically renovated 1920s Art Deco former textile factory, and well situated for the cafés and bars of the Spui neighbourhood. Some of the rooms have canal views, and all boast extremely comfy beds and good showers. Breakfast included. €€€

The Grachtengordel

AMBASSADE MAP PAGE 44, POCKET MAP A13. **Herengracht 341.** ⓦ **ambassade-hotel.nl.** Eminently appealing hotel, probably the city's best, that occupies a series of cleverly renovated seventeenth-century canal houses. There are fifty-six guest rooms in total, each decorated in period-meets-country-house style, mostly in pastel shades and with luxurious beds and high-spec bathrooms. There's also a well-stocked library – it's a very classy place - and prize modern art throughout. Breakfast is taken in an elegant panelled room. €€€€

BACKSTAGE HOTEL MAP PAGE 44, POCKET MAP B5. **Leidsegracht 114.** ⓦ **backstagehotel.com.** This hotel is primarily aimed at musicians playing at the nearby *Melkweg* and *Paradiso*, and furnishings like theatre mirrors, spotlights and flight cases in the 22 rooms are designed to make them feel at home. Everyone can enjoy the 24hr bar and pool table. €€

CLEMENS MAP PAGE 44, POCKET MAP C3. **Raadhuisstraat 39.** ⓦ **clemenshotel.nl.** Well-run two-star budget hotel with tidy modern rooms in a handy location close to the Anne Frank Huis. One of the better options along this busy main road. All rooms are en suite and have flatscreen TVs and a/c. €

DIKKER & THIJS FENICE MAP PAGE 44, POCKET MAP C5. **Prinsengracht 444.** ⓦ **dikkerandthijshotelamsterdam.com.** Small and stylish hotel not far from Leidseplein. Rooms vary in decor but are brisk and modern in demeanour and some have canal views. Those on the top floor have good views of the city. €€€

DYLAN MAP PAGE 44, POCKET MAP C4. **Keizersgracht 384.** ⓦ **dylanamsterdam.com.** One of Amsterdam's most luxurious hotels, housed in a seventeenth-century building that centres on a beautiful courtyard and terrace. Boutique in size and style, its forty sumptuous rooms range from opulent reds or greens to minimal white decor. The hotel restaurant offers tip-top French cuisine and the bar is open to non-guests. €€€€

ESTHEREA MAP PAGE 44, POCKET MAP A13. **Singel 303–309.** ⓦ **estherea.nl.** Comfortable, sometimes sedate, four-star hotel converted from a couple of sympathetically modernized canal houses. There's no hankering after minimalism here, with thick, plush carpets and beds that you literally sink into. €€€€

HEGRA BY STANLEY COLLECTION MAP PAGE 44, POCKET MAP A13. **Herengracht 269.** ⓦ **stanley-hotels.com.** On a handsome stretch of canal near the Spui, this hotel has a welcoming atmosphere and neat and trim modern rooms. The rooms with a canal view are a slab more expensive than the others. €€€€

'T HOTEL MAP PAGE 44, POCKET MAP A11. **Leliegracht 18.** ⓦ **thotel.nl.** Appealing hotel located in an old high-gabled house along a quiet stretch of canal. The eight spacious rooms are decorated in a bright, cheerful style with large beds and either a bath or shower. €€€

THE HOXTON MAP PAGE 44, POCKET MAP A12. **Herengracht 255.** ⓦ **thehoxton.com.** This distinctive hotel, the first opening outside London of this hipster-cool mini-chain, occupies several conjoined canal houses in a prime location. The public rooms have a bustling vibe and a semi-industrial feel with brown and white tiling - and the guest rooms continue in the same style. They range from the snug ("Shoebox") to the slightly more roomy ("Cosy") and then the more spacious ("Roomy"). €€€€

HOTEL SEVEN ONE SEVEN MAP PAGE 44, POCKET MAP C5. **Prinsengracht 717.** ⓦ **717hotel.nl.** Deluxe canal house hotel with just nine suites, all individually designed. Great, large spaces, lovingly conceived, and one of the most luxurious small hotels in the city. €€€€

MAISON RIKA MAP PAGE 44, POCKET MAP A13. **Oude Spiegelstraat 12.** ⓦ **maison-rika.hoteleamsterdam.net.** Housed in a former art gallery, this boutique option offers two beautifully furnished bedrooms on the second and third floors and is owned by a local fashion designer. There's free water, chocolates, tea and coffee, but no breakfast. €€€€

MARCEL'S CREATIVE EXCHANGE MAP PAGE 44, POCKET MAP C5. **Leidsestraat 87.** ⓦ **marcelamsterdam.nl.** Named after the owner, a talented graphic designer and artist, this stylishly restored house is a relaxing and appealing haven with regulars returning year after year. Offers three en-suite doubles, a suite and the decor is chic and enticing. You'll need to book well in advance. Breakfast isn't included, but there are tea- and coffee-making facilities. €€€

MAX BROWN HOTEL CANAL DISTRICT MAP PAGE 44, POCKET MAP B10. **Herengracht 13.** ⓦ **maxbrownhotels.com.** Chic boutique hotel with a playful stylish air and lots of modern art to gaze and gawp at. Has twenty-odd appealing, if not always especially spacious rooms, some overlooking the canal. The changeable lighting allows you to adjust the colour of your room according to your mood – a gimmick perhaps, but an effective one. €€€

THE PAVILIONS AMSTERDAM TOREN MAP PAGE 44, POCKET MAP C3. **Keizersgracht 164.** ⓦ **pavilionshotels.com.** Swish, retro-chic boutique hotel, converted from two elegant canal houses. All rooms have been renovated, some have large jacuzzis and there's also an annexe. There's a sumptuous bar/breakfast room downstairs. Lavish in the extreme. €€€€

PRINSENHOF MAP PAGE 44, POCKET MAP E6. **Prinsengracht 810.** ⓦ **prinsenhof.amsterdam.com.** Tastefully decorated, this is one of the city's top budget options, a one-star hotel with just eleven simple but spick and span guest rooms. Advance booking essential. €€

SEVEN BRIDGES MAP PAGE 44, POCKET MAP E5. **Reguliersgracht 31.** ⓦ **sevenbridgeshotel.nl.** Very charming place – and excellent value for money. It takes its name from its canalside location, which affords a view of seven dinky little bridges. Beautifully decorated in an antique style, its spotless rooms are regularly revamped. Small and popular, so reservations are pretty much essential. Breakfast is included in the price and served in your room. €€€

SINGEL HOTEL MAP PAGE 44, POCKET MAP B10. **Singel 13–17.** ⓦ **singelhotel.nl.** Pleasant hotel located in three charming canal houses right next to the old Lutheran church. The rooms are rather small and functional, but well equipped, and some overlook the canal. €€

WEBER MAP PAGE 44 POCKET MAP B5. **Marnixstraat 397.** **hotelweber.nl.** Boutique hotel with seven spacious rooms kitted out in a sleek, modern style. The hotel is above a popular bar. Small in-room breakfast provided. €€

WIECHMANN MAP PAGE 44, POCKET MAP C4. **Prinsengracht 328–332.** **hotelwiechmann.nl.** Family-run for over fifty years, this mid-sized hotel occupies an old canal house close to the Anne Frank Huis. The décor throughout is very traditional, but there are bright moments – like the antique wooden beams of some of the ceilings. The guest rooms are a tad spartan, but the pick are large and bright and in good condition. €€

The Old Jewish Quarter and Plantage

MONET GARDEN HOTEL MAP PAGE 70, POCKET MAP F4. **Valkenburgerstraat 76.** **monetgardenhotelamsterdam.com.** In a straightforward modern block beside a boulevard, this is a very appealing mid-range hotel, where the better rooms at the back have canal views. All the guest rooms are neat, trim and modern. €€€

The eastern docklands and Amsterdam Noord

CRANE HOTEL FARALDA MAP PAGE 82, POCKET MAP E1. NDSM-**Plein 78.** **faralda.com.** Probably the world's first hotel in a one-time industrial crane – it used to be part of the NDSM shipyard – offering three ultra-contemporary suites with knee-buckling city views. There's even a spa pool. As you might expect, there's a long waiting list, so book well in advance. €€€€

HOTEL JAKARTA MAP PAGE 80, POCKET MAP H2. **Javakade 766.** **hoteljakarta.amsterdam.** Perhaps no particular structure epitomises the vaunting ambition behind the redevelopment of the eastern docklands more than this luxury hotel, a translucent edifice whose glassy public areas abound with palm and bamboo trees. Similarly, the décor of the two hundred rooms and suites beyond is inspired by Indonesia. €€€€

LLOYD HOTEL MAP PAGE 80, POCKET MAP H3. **Oostelijke Handelskade 34.** **lloydhotel.com.** Situated in the up-and-coming Oosterdok district, this former workers' hostel has been renovated to become one of Amsterdam's coolest hotels. Rather pretentiously subtitled a "cultural embassy" (it has an arts centre and library), the rooms range from one-star affairs to five-star offerings. Some rooms are great, others not so – don't be afraid to ask to change. €€€

The Museum Quarter and around

CATALONIA VONDEL MAP PAGE 90, POCKET MAP B6. **Vondelstraat 26.** **cataloniahotels.com.** Part of a small chain of design-conscious boutique hotels, this place is as cool as its cousins, with black paint and light natural wood characterizing the guest rooms. There's a pleasant bar and breakfast room and modern art decorates the walls of the common areas. Doubles vary considerably in size. €€€

COLLEGE MAP PAGE 90, POCKET MAP C8. **Roelof Hartstraat 1.** **thecollegehotel.com.** Converted from an old schoolhouse, the *College* is one of the most inventive additions to Amsterdam's hotel scene. Original because it's largely run by students from the city's catering school; elegant because of the sheer class of the refurbishment. €€€

CONSCIOUS HOTEL MUSEUM SQUARE MAP PAGE 90, POCKET MAP B8. **De Lairessestraat 7.** **conscioushotels.com.** This medium-sized hotel is proud of being one hundred percent sustainable, from the living plant wall by reception to the guest rooms, which feature photographic forest wallpaper, desks made out of recycled yoghurt pots, and ergonomic beds. Other pluses are the scrumptious organic breakfast, bike rental and hotel garden. €€€

CONSERVATORIUM MAP PAGE 90, POCKET MAP B7. **Paulus Potterstraat 50.** **conservatoriumhotel.com.** Arguably the city's most jaw-dropping hotel, this heritage building – once a Conservatorium – has been transformed into a contemporary design wonderland. Standard guestrooms come with access to Akasha – the city's largest and most opulent spa. €€€€

DE HALLEN MAP PAGE 90, POCKET MAP A4. **Bellamyplein 47.** ⓦ **hoteldehallen.com.** Medium-sized hotel shoehorned into an immaculately revamped old tram depot from 1902. Original features have been kept and the small but smart rooms spread over two floors and round a central atrium. Great, buzzy atmosphere, too. €€€€

HOTEL AMSTERDAM – BILDERBERG GARDEN HOTEL MAP PAGE 90, POCKET MAP A9. **Dijsselhofplantsoen 7.** ⓦ **bilderberg.nl/hotels/garden-hotel/.** Sleek, modern hotel located in a quiet area of Amsterdam. It's an ideal base for visiting the Museum Quarter and it's within walking distance of Vondelpark. The rooms are clean and contemporary, featuring large, comfortable beds. Good buffet breakfast too. Double rooms €€

ROEMER MAP PAGE 90, POCKET MAP B6. **Roemer Visscherstraat 10.** ⓦ **hotelroemer.com.** Immaculate, four-star hotel in an extensively revamped old mansion, whose dignified red-brick exterior is repeated in the large houses that run along the whole of this side-street. There's a pleasant garden out the back and although the rooms vary considerably in terms of both comfort and aesthetics, they are all neat and modern. €€€

De Pijp, Nieuw Zuid and Amsterdam Oost

HOTEL ARENA MAP PAGE 100, POCKET MAP H6. **Gravesandestraat 55.** ⓦ **hotelarena.nl.** A little way east of the centre, in a renovated old orphanage on the edge of the Oosterpark, this place has been thoroughly revamped, transforming a popular hostel into a hip three-star hotel complete with split-level rooms and minimalist decor. Despite the odd pretentious flourish, it manages to retain a relaxed vibe attracting both businesspeople and travellers alike. €€€

BICYCLE HOTEL MAP PAGE 96, POCKET MAP D8. **Van Ostadestraat 123.** ⓣ **020 679 3452,** ⓦ **bicyclehotel.com. Metro #52 from Centraal Station to De Pijp.** Friendly place down a quiet residential street, not far from the Albert Cuyp market in De Pijp. It bills itself as the "bicycle hotel", renting bikes and giving advice on routes and such like. Garage parking availabl. Basic but clean en suite two-, three- and four-bed rooms, with cheaper rates for shared facilities. €

MET HOTEL AMSTERDAM MAP PAGE 100, POCKET MAP A5. **Marius Bauerstraat 401.** ⓦ **methotelamsterdam.com.** Slightly out of town in a quiet, upmarket neighbourhood, but with excellent metro, bus and tram connections. It's a perfect base for exploring the city in comfort, it features modern, well-appointed rooms, attractive bar and restaurant and a superb breakfast buffet. €€

HOTEL OKURA MAP PAGE 96, POCKET MAP D9. **Ferdinand Bolstraat 333.** ⓦ **okura.nl.** Don't be fooled by the concrete, purpose-built facade - this deluxe five-star hotel comes equipped with all the luxuries you would expect. Rooms have huge marble bathrooms, and, in the suites, mood lighting and control units for the curtains. Two of its four restaurants have Michelin stars. €€€€

VOLKSHOTEL MAP PAGE 100, POCKET MAP G8. **Wibautstraat 150.** ⓦ **volkshotel.nl.** Opened in the former offices of the Dutch newspaper *De Volkskrant*, this place really does do what it says on the tin, with cheap rates and great views from most of its 172 rooms, which were designed according to nine different, somewhat wacky concepts. Other perks include a rooftop sauna and hot tub. €€

Hostels

When it comes to accommodation, the least expensive option is to take a dorm bed in a hostel – and there are a number to choose from: Hostelling International places, unofficial private hostels, even boutique-stye hostels. Most hostels will provide (relatively) clean bed linen or charge a few euros for it as they usually do for issuing a towel. Many hostels also lock guests out for a short period each day to clean the place, and some set a nightly curfew. Most provide some sort of basic breakfast too.

The Old Centre

FLYING PIG DOWNTOWN MAP PAGE 26, POCKET MAP C11. **Nieuwendijk 100. ⓦ flyingpig.nl.** Clean, large and well run by ex-travellers. Free use of kitchen facilities, no curfew, plus there's a late-night coffeeshop next door and the hostel bar is open all night. Justifiably popular, and a very good deal, with both mixed and single-sex dorm beds as well as private double and single rooms. Dorm beds €; double rooms €€

STAYOKAY STADSDOELEN MAP PAGE 26, POCKET MAP C13. **Kloveniersburgwal 97. ⓦ stayokay.com.** The closest to Centraal Station of the two official hostels, with clean, semi-private dorms and double rooms. Price includes linen, breakfast and locker, plus use of the communal kitchen. The bar overlooks the canal and serves good-value if basic food. See also the city's other HI hostel, the *Stay Okay Vondelpark*, which has a greater choice of rooms.Dorm beds €; double rooms €€

WINSTON HOSTEL MAP PAGE 26, POCKET MAP C12. **Warmoesstraat 129. ⓦ winston.nl.** This self-consciously young and cool hostel-cum-hotel has funky rooms decorated with crazy art, and a busy ground-floor bar that has regular live music. It's a formula that works a treat; the *Winston* is often full – though this is probably also due to its low prices, which include breakfast. Dorm beds €; double rooms €€

The Grachtengordel

COCOMAMA MAP PAGE 44, POCKET MAP E7. **Westeinde 18. ⓣ 31206272454.** This hotel-hostel is excellently located. The ground floor emphasizes the hostel vibe with its communal kitchen and has a nice mix of small dorms, while the private en-suite doubles on the upper levels would not be out of place in a boutique hotel. Dorm beds €, double rooms €€

HANS BRINKER MAP PAGE 44, POCKET MAP C5. **Kerkstraat 136–138. ⓦ hansbrinker.com.** Well-established and raucously popular Amsterdam hostel, with several hundred beds. The four- to eight-bed dorms are basic and clean. The facilities are good: free internet, disco most nights, and it's near to the buzz of Leidseplein too. A hostel to head for if you're out for a good time (and not too bothered about getting a solid night's sleep). Dorm beds €; double rooms €€

The Old Jewish Quarter and Plantage

ECOMAMA MAP PAGE 70, POCKET MAP F4. **Valkenburgerstraat 124. ⓦ ecomamahotel.com.** Superb eco-hostel with a green roof, water-saving system and rooms that range from "El Cheapo" twelve-bed dorms to very stylish private en-suite doubles; there's a women's-only dorm too. Dorm beds €; double rooms €€

Amsterdam Noord

CLINKNOORD MAP PAGE 82, POCKET MAP F1. **Badhuiskade 3. ⓦ clinkhostels.com.** Take the free passenger ferry from behind Centraal Station to the Eye Film Institute & the hostel is a 2min walk from the dock. Perhaps the city's most unusual hostel, occupying part of the former headquarters of Shell, in a sterling office block dating from the 1920s. Has four- to ten-bunk dorms, some women only, as well as private doubles. Facilities include a free cinema, self-catering kitchen, café and library, plus a bar with live music. Dorm beds €; double rooms €€

The Museum Quarter and around

FLYING PIG UPTOWN MAP PAGE 90, POCKET MAP B6. **Vossiusstraat 46. ⓦ flyingpig.nl.** The better of the two *Flying Pig* hostels, facing the Vondelpark and close to the city's most important museums. Immaculate and well maintained by a staff of travellers, who understand their backpacking guests. Free use of kitchen facilities and no curfew. Single and double bunk beds in small to medium-sized dorms plus private singles and doubles. Dorm beds €; Double rooms €€

ESSENTIALS

Cycling in Amsterdam

Arrival

Arriving in Amsterdam by train and plane could hardly be easier. Amsterdam's one and only international **airport** is a quick and convenient train ride away from the city's **principal train station**, which stands at the heart of the city. Most long-distance buses arrive at the airport, too.

By air

Amsterdam's sprawling international airport, **Schiphol** (ⓦ schiphol.nl), is located about 17km southwest of the city centre. Trains run from the airport to Amsterdam Centraal Station every ten minutes during the day, every hour at night (midnight–6am); the journey takes 15–20 minutes and costs just a few euros. Taxi fares from Schiphol to most parts of the city centre are €45–50. The Connexxion bus service (ⓦ connexxion.nl) departs from the designated bus stop outside the Arrivals Hall every thirty minutes or so from 6am to 9pm. The route varies with the needs of the passengers it picks up at the airport, but buses take about forty minutes to get from the airport to the city centre. Tickets are bought either online or at the Connexxion desk in the Arrivals Hall.

By train

Amsterdam's **Centraal Station** (CS) has regular connections with key cities in Germany, Belgium and France, as well as all the larger towns and cities of the Netherlands. Eurostar (ⓦ eurostar.com) operates an excellent and rapid direct service from London St Pancras to Amsterdam Centraal with several departures daily. With global warming in mind – try to take the train rather than the plane. Amsterdam also has several suburban train stations, but these are principally for commuters. For all rail enquiries consult **NS** (Netherlands Railways; ⓦ ns.nl).

By bus

Flixbus (ⓦ flixbus.co.uk) long-distance, international buses from a range of European cities, including London, arrive at Schiphol airport.

City transport

Almost all of Amsterdam's leading attractions are within easy walking distance of each other, but the city does have a first-rate public transport system, run by **GVB** (ⓦ gvb.nl). Centraal Station is the hub of the system, with trams and buses departing from outside on Stationsplein, which is also the location of a metro station and a GVB public transport information office. There's a taxi rank on Stationsplein too.

Tickets

The **OV-Chipkaart** (ⓦ ov-chipkaart.nl) is an electronic payment card which covers the cost of travelling on all of the GVB transport system. There are two main sorts of card – rechargeable plastic cards and disposable paper cards set to a predetermined value and length of time. Disposable cards are best for short stays. Cards are sold at the tourist office and on the city's trams and at the metro. You must scan the card when you get on and off the bus, tram, ferry or metro. A disposable *dagkaart* (day ticket), for unlimited travel, costs €8.50 for 24 hours, €14.50 for 48 hours and €20 for 72 hours; these day tickets do not cover the train ride from the city to the airport.

Trams, metro and buses

Trams criss-cross the city and are the most agreeable way to explore Amsterdam. **Buses** are mainly useful for going to the outskirts, and the same applies to the **metro**, which has a handful of city-centre stations. Trams, buses and the metro operate daily between 6am and midnight, supplemented by a limited number of night buses (*nachtbussen*). All central tram and bus stops display a detailed map of the network. For further details on all services, head for the main GVB information office on Stationsplein (Mon–Fri 7am–9pm, Sat & Sun 10am–6pm; gvb.nl). Its free, English-language, public transport information booklet is very helpful, and includes a free transport map. You can download the GVB app and purchase a ticket for 1, 24, 28, 72, 96 or 120 hours of travel which covers all GVB trams, buses, night buses and metros. Just scan the QR code when you board your chosen transport.

Hop-on, hop-off canal boats

One good way to get around Amsterdam's waterways is to take a **Hop-on, Hop-off boat** (lovers.nl). These operate on two circular routes, an outer loop coloured green and an inner route coloured red, which meet at various places. There are fourteen stops in all and together they give easy access to all the major sights. Boats leave from opposite Centraal Station every half an hour or so during low season between 10am and 5.30pm (longer in high season), and a 24hr ticket for both routes, allowing you to hop on and off as many times as you like, costs around €29.50 per adult, €14.75 for children (4–11 years old).

Canal boat tours

A platoon of **boat tour** operators line up outside Centraal Station. **Prices** are fairly uniform with a one-hour canal tour costing around €16 per adult, €8 per child (4–12 years old), and around €20–25 for a two-hour cruise at night. The big companies also offer more **specialized boat trips** – dinner cruises, literary cruises, and so forth. All these cruises are popular and long queues are common in the summer. One way of avoiding much of the crush is to walk down the Damrak from Centraal Station to the jetty at the south end of the Rokin, where the first-rate Reederij P. Kooij (rederijkooij.nl) offers all the basic cruises at competitive prices.

Bicycles

The city has an excellent network of designated bicycle lanes (*fietspaden*). The needs of the cyclist take precedence over those of the motorist and by law, if there's a collision, it's always the driver's fault. Bike rental is straightforward. There are lots of **rental companies** (*fietsenverhuur*) but MacBike (macbike.nl) is perhaps the most convenient, with several rental

Tour operators

Gilde Amsterdam 020 625 4450, gildeamsterdam.nl. Guided walking tours of several different types by long-time – and often older – Amsterdam residents. Tours run daily except Monday; the city-centre tour costs €11 per person. Advance reservations (at least 24hr) are required.

Yellow Bike Tours Nieuwezijds Kolk 29, off Nieuwezijds Voorburgwal 020 620 6940, yellowbike.nl. Two-hour guided cycling tours around the city (1–2 daily) that cost €29 per person, including the bike. Advance reservations required.

outlets in central Amsterdam, including one at Centraal Station and another on Waterlooplein. They charge €13.50 for three hours or €17.50 per day for a standard bicycle; 21-speed cycles cost about half as much. All bike rental companies ask for some type of deposit.

Taxis

The centre of Amsterdam is geared up for trams and bicycles rather than cars, so **taxis** are not used as much as they are in many other cities. They are, however, plentiful: taxi ranks are all over the city centre and they can also be hailed on the street. **Fares** are metered and reasonably high, but city distances are small: the trip from Centraal Station to the Leidseplein, for example, will cost around €15, €4 more to Museumplein – and about fifteen percent more late at night.

Directory A–Z

Accessible travel

In Amsterdam, visitors with mobility concerns will find the cobbled streets and narrow pavements of the city centre a real issue. Provision on public transport is fairly limited too, though all public buildings are required to provide access – and do.

Addresses

Addresses are written as, for example, "Kerkstr.79 II", which means the second-floor apartment at Kerkstraat 79. The ground floor is indicated by *hs* (*huis*, house) after the number; the basement is *sous* (souterrain). In some cases 1e, 2e, 3e and 4e are placed in front of street addresses; these are abbreviations for *Eerste* (first), *Tweede* (second), *Derde* (third) and *Vierde* (fourth). Many side streets take the name of the street they run off, with the addition of the word *dwars*, meaning "crossing"– for instance, Palmdwarsstraat is a side street off Palmstraat. The main Grachtengordel canals begin their numbering at Brouwersgracht and increase as they progress anticlockwise. T/O (*tegenover* or "opposite") shows that the address is a boat.

Children

In general terms at least, Dutch society is sympathetic to (well-behaved) children and so is the tourist industry. Concessions are commonplace, from public transport through to museums, and so are children's menus at cafés and restaurants. Baby-changing stations are common too.

Cinema

Most of Amsterdam's commercial **cinemas** are multiplexes showing general releases, but there's also a scattering of film houses showing revival and art films and occasional retrospectives. The **Kriterion** at Roeterstraat 170 (T 020 623 1708, W kriterion.nl) is a stylish cinema close to the Weesperplein metro that shows arthouse and quality commercial films, while the beautiful Art Deco cinema **The Movies**, at Haarlemmerdijk 159 (T 020 638 6016, W themovies.nl), shows independent films. The Eye Film Institute (see page 83), across the River IJ from Centraal Station, offers an ambitious programme of independent, cult and vintage films.

Crime and emergencies

Although Amsterdam is relatively safe and free from serious crime when compared to other European capitals, do be on your guard against petty crime, especially pickpockets.

Emergency numbers

For the police, fire service and ambulance call ⓣ 112.

Cyclists should always lock their bikes when they leave them as bike theft is something of a local industry. If you are robbed, go to the police, who are characteristically helpful and usually speak English.

Discount passes

Given that most of the city's key attractions are very expensive (€15 and counting), a discount pass is likely to save you a fair wad of euros. The best pass is the **I amsterdam City Card** (ⓦ iamsterdam.com), which provides free and unlimited use of the city's public transport network, a complimentary canal cruise and free admission to the bulk of the city's museums and attractions. It costs €65 for one day, €90 for two consecutive days, €110 for three consecutive days, and €125 for four consecutive days. There are also regular if modest discounts on these prices if you purchase online. An alternative, if you're staying for more than a week or so, is the outstanding-value **Museumkaart** (ⓦ museumkaart.nl), which gives free entry to almost every museum in the whole of the Netherlands for a year; it costs €75, or €39 for under-19s.

Drugs

Drugs, both hard and soft, are **illegal** in the Netherlands, though the country has long tolerated the consumption of small amounts of cannabis (under 5g) in designated premises (coffeeshops). In recent years there have been proposals to limit access to coffeeshops to non-Dutch citizens, though in Amsterdam this has not yet happened and maybe never will. Other soft drugs including magic mushrooms and "space cakes" are illegal.

Electricity

The Dutch electricity supply runs at 220V AC. British equipment needs only a plug adaptor; American apparatus requires a transformer and an adaptor.

Embassies and consulates

Australia Carnegielaan 4, 2517 KH The Hague ⓣ 070 310 8200; **Canada** Sophialaan 7, 2514 JP The Hague ⓣ 070 311 1600; **Ireland** Scheveningseweg 112, 2584 AE The Hague ⓣ 070 363 0993; **New Zealand** Eisenhowerlaan 77N, 2517 KK The Hague ⓣ 070 346 9324; **South Africa** Wassenaarseweg 40, 2596 CJ The Hague ⓣ 070 392 4501; **UK** Lange Voorhout 10, 2514 ED The Hague ⓣ 070 427 0427; **USA** John Adams Park 1, 2244 BZ Wassenaar, The Hague ⓣ 070 310 2209.

Health

Your hotel should be able to provide the address of an English-speaking doctor or dentist if you need one. Otherwise call the emergency number ⓣ 112. **Minor ailments** can be remedied at a drugstore (*drogist*). These sell non-prescription drugs as well as toiletries, tampons, condoms and the like. Pharmacies or *apotheeks* (usually open Mon–Fri 9.30am–6pm, but often closed Mon mornings) also handle prescriptions; centrally located pharmacies include Dam Apotheek (Damstraat 2 ⓣ 020 624 4331) and Apotheek Koek, Schaeffer & Van Tijen (Vijzelgracht 19 ⓣ 020 623 5949).

Left luggage

Centraal Station has card-only luggage lockers (daily 5am–midnight).

LGBTQ+ Amsterdam

Amsterdam is one of the top LGBTQ+ destinations in Europe: attitudes are tolerant, bars are excellent and support groups and facilities are unequalled. The age of consent is 16. Consider timing your visit to coincide with Amsterdam Pride (amsterdamgaypride.nl) on the first weekend of August.

Lost property

For items lost on GVB trams, buses or the metro, go to their website (gvb.nl/en/customer-service/lost-found), where they post photos of lost possessions. For items lost on an NS train, go to the ticket office at the nearest station within five days, after which it is bundled up and sent to the Centraal Bureau Gevonden Voorwerpen (Central Lost Property Office) in Utrecht.

Money

Debit cards are now the norm, and most shops and restaurants accept these and all major credit cards. You'll find ATMs throughout the city. Bureaux de change are also scattered around town – GWK Travelex has 24-hour branches at Centraal Station and Schiphol airport.

Opening hours

The Dutch weekend fades painlessly into the working week, with many smaller shops and businesses staying closed on Monday mornings until noon. Normal shop opening hours are, however, Monday to Saturday 9am to 6pm and Sunday noon to 5pm. Many places also stay open late on Thursday evenings.

Most **restaurants** are open for dinner from about 5.30pm or 6pm, and though some close as early as 9.30pm, 10.30pm or 11pm is more usual. Bars, cafés and coffeeshops are either open all day from around 10am or don't open until about 5pm; most close at 1am during the week and 2am at weekends. Nightclubs generally open their doors from 11pm to 4am during the week, though very few open every night, and some stay open until 5am at the weekend. **Museums and galleries** are usually open from Monday to Friday from 10am to 5pm and from 11am to 5pm on weekends, but some close on Mondays. Note that both the Anne Frank Huis (see page 46) and the Van Gogh Museum (see page 89) only allow entry on prebooked, timed tickets.

Phones

The international phone code for the Netherlands is 31. Numbers prefixed 0800 are free; those prefixed 0900 are premium-rated – a (Dutch) message before you're connected tells you how much you will be paying for the call, and you can only call them from within the Netherlands. There is good coverage for **mobile phones/cell phones** all over Amsterdam. Prepaid SIM cards are available in

Eating out price codes

All the **cafés and restaurants** detailed in this Guide has been graded according to the four price categories listed below. These represent how much you can expect to pay in each establishment for a **two-course meal for one including a drink** excluding special deals and discounts.

€ = €20–25
€€ = €25–35
€€€ = €35–45
€€€€ = €45+

telephone shops (on the Rokin and around Kalverstraat) and in some supermarkets. The Dutch phone directory is available (in Dutch) at Ⓦ detelefoongids.nl.

Post

The privatized Dutch postal service is branded as PostNL (Ⓦ postnl.nl). Stamps are sold at supermarkets, shops and hotels.

Smoking

Smoking (tobacco) is banned in many public places as well as in all restaurants, cafés and bars and even, oddly enough, in coffeeshops.

Time

The Netherlands is on Central European Time (CET), one hour ahead of UK time and six hours ahead of EST in the USA. Daylight saving operates from the end of March to the end of October.

Tipping

You are expected to leave a tip if you have enjoyed good service – up to around ten percent of the bill should suffice in restaurants, while taxi drivers expect a euro or two on top of the fare.

Tourist information

Amsterdam's main tourist information office, branded *I Amsterdam*, is straight across from the main train station entrance on Stationsplein (daily 9am–5pm; Ⓦ iamsterdam.com). They sell a range of maps and guidebooks. They also take in-person bookings for canal cruises and other tours, supply theatre and concert tickets, and sell the I Amsterdam discount pass (see page 125). There is a second I Amsterdam information office at the back of the train station down near the River IJ (Mon–Fri 9am–5pm).

Festivals and events

Stille Omgang (Silent Procession)

Sun closest to March 15 Ⓦ stille-omgang.nl.

Procession by local Catholics commemorating the Miracle of Amsterdam, starting and finishing at Spui.

Koningsdag (King's Day)

April 27

The highlight of the festival calendar: a celebration of the King's birthday, with the entire city centre given over to one massive party (in orange).

Herdenkingsdag (Remembrance Day)

May 4

Wreath-laying ceremony and two-minute silence at the National Monument in Dam Square to commemorate the Dutch who died in World War II.

Bevrijdingsdag (Liberation Day)

May 5

The country celebrates the 1945 liberation from German occupation with bands, speeches and impromptu markets around the city.

Holland Festival

Throughout June Ⓦ hollandfestival.nl.

The largest music, dance and drama event in the Netherlands, showcasing productions at venues around the city.

Nomads Festival

Late June Ⓦ nomadsfestival.nl.

Hugely popular house music festival with its own organic market and

Arabian-style chill-out lounge. Tickets sell out fast.

Vondelpark Open Air Theatre

Mid-June to Aug Fri–Sun only **openluchttheater.nl.** Free theatre, dance and music performances throughout the summer, presenting anything from jazz and classical concerts through to stand-up comedy.

Julidans

First half of July **julidans.nl.** Fourteen-day festival dedicated to contemporary dance. It is held in numerous locations around the Leidseplein, with the Stadsschouwburg as its throbbing heart.

Cannabis Cup

Mid-July **cannabiscup.com.** Three-day event celebrating and judging new strains, with seminars, tours and music events. Venues include several coffeeshops and the Melkweg, which also hosts a competition to find the best cultivated seed. Recently moved to July from its traditional date in November.

Amsterdam Pride

First weekend of Aug **amsterdamgaypride.nl.** The city's flourishing LGBTQ+ community celebrates with street parties held along the Amstel, Warmoesstraat and Reguliersdwarsstraat.

Grachtenfestival

Ten days in mid-Aug **grachtenfestival.nl.** International musicians perform at over ninety classical music events at historical locations around the three main canals, as well as beside the River IJ.

Uitmarkt

Last weekend in Aug **uitmarkt.nl.** Every cultural organization in the city, from opera to theatre, advertises its forthcoming programme of events with free preview performances held around the Museumplein and Leidseplein.

Open Monument Day

Second weekend in Sept **openmonumentendag.nl.** Over the course of a weekend, monuments throughout the Netherlands that are normally closed or have restricted opening times, throw open their doors to the public for free.

The Jordaan Festival

Second or third weekend in Sept **jordaanfestival.nl.** A three-day street festival in the Jordaan. There's a commercial fair on Palmgracht, talent contests on

Public holidays

January 1 New Year's Day
Good Friday (although many shops open)
Easter Sunday
Easter Monday
April 27 King's Day
May 5 Liberation Day
Ascension Day (40 days after Easter)
Whit Sunday and Monday
December 25 and 26 Christmas

Elandsgracht, a few street parties and a culinary fair on the Sunday afternoon at the Noordermarkt.

Amsterdam Dance Festival

Late Oct
amsterdam-dance-event.nl.
A five-day dance music festival, hosting hundreds of national and international DJs taking over venues across the city. Tickets for all events have to be purchased separately and tend to sell out quickly.

Imagine Film Festival

Late Oct to early Nov
imaginefilmfestival.nl.
A mix of features and short films hosted across the city, including The Eye, ranging from science fiction to horror, produced by both Dutch and foreign directors. Look out for the Night of Terror event held normally at the Tuschinski cinema.

Museum Night

Sat in early Nov
museumnacht.amsterdam.
A great opportunity to explore Amsterdam's museums in the early hours. Most museums are open until 2am, hosting DJ performances, workshops and concerts.

Parade of Sint Nicolaas

Second or third Sun in Nov
sintinamsterdam.nl
The traditional parade of *Sinterklaas* (Santa Claus) begins with his arrival by steam boat, which chugs its way through the city to dock at the Scheepvaartmuseum (Maritime Museum). Thereafter, the bearded one progresses through the city on his white horse to finish up at the Dam.

Pakjesavond (Present Evening)

Dec 5
Though it tends to be a private affair, Pakjesavond, rather than Christmas Day, is when Dutch kids receive their Christmas presents.

New Year's Eve

Dec 31
Fireworks and celebrations are everywhere, and most bars and clubs stay open until early morning. This might just qualify as the wildest street partying in Europe.

Chronology

1200s Amsterdam begins to prosper.

1425 Digging of the Singel, Amsterdam's first horseshoe-shaped canal.

1530s Inspired by Martin Luther and subsequently Calvin, Protestantism takes root.

1555 The fanatically Catholic Habsburg Philip II becomes king of Spain and ruler of the Low Countries, including Amsterdam. Philip prepares to bring his heretical subjects to heel.

1566 The Protestants strike back, purging churches of their "papist" reliquaries and shrines.

1567 Philip dispatches a huge army to the Low Countries to suppress his religious opponents; the preeminent Protestant leader is William the Silent, Prince William of Orange-Nassau.

1578 Amsterdam deserts the Spanish cause and declares for William, switching from Catholicism to Calvinism at the same time.

1579 The seven northern provinces of the Low Countries sign the Union of Utrecht, an alliance against Spain that is the first unification of the Netherlands; the signees call themselves the United Provinces. The Spanish Netherlands (now Belgium) remain under Habsburg control.

17th century The Golden Age. Amsterdam becomes the emporium for the products of Europe as well as the East and West Indies. By the middle of the century Amsterdam's wealth is spectacular.

1613 Enlargement of Amsterdam begins with the digging of the three great canals of the Grachtengordel.

1648 Peace with Spain; Dutch independence is recognized.

1672 William III of Orange becomes ruler of the United Provinces.

1770–1790 Amsterdam is split into two opposing factions – the Orangists (supporters of the House of Orange) and the Patriots (who are pro-French).

1795 The French army occupies the United Provinces. Many of the Dutch elite's privileges are removed.

1814 After Napoleon's defeat at Waterloo, Frederick William of Orange-Nassau is crowned King William I of the United Kingdom of the Netherlands, incorporating both the United Provinces and the former Spanish Netherlands (Belgium). The seat of government becomes Den Haag (The Hague).

1830 The provinces of what had been the Spanish Netherlands revolt against Frederick William and establish the separate Kingdom of Belgium. Amsterdam stagnates.

1914–18 The Netherlands remains neutral during World War I.

1940 In World War II, the Germans overrun the Netherlands.

1941 The Germans start rounding up and deporting the city's Jews in earnest.

1942 Anne Frank plus family and friends hide away in the back annexe in the Prinsengracht.

1944 Betrayal and capture of the Franks; Anne dies in Belsen concentration camp, but her father – Otto – survives the war and publishes his daughter's diary in 1947.

May 1945 The Allies liberate Amsterdam, but many die of starvation during the hunger winter of 1945-6.

1960s Amsterdam changes from a conservative city into a hotbed of hippy happenings.

1976 The Netherlands decriminalizes the possession of soft drugs, principally cannabis. The first dope-selling "coffeeshops" open.

Late 1970s Amsterdam's squatter movement booms.

1984 The squatting movement has a series of major showdowns with the police. There are mass riots.

Late 1980s The squatter movement fizzles out.

1990s Several huge redevelopment schemes are planned, most notably among the old docklands bordering the River IJ.

1992 An El Al cargo plane crashes into Amsterdam's Bijlmermeer housing estate, killing 43 people.

2000 The Dutch parliament repeals the laws prohibiting brothels.

2001 The Netherlands becomes the first country in the world to recognize gay marriage.

2002 The guilder is replaced by the euro.

2004 Filmmaker Theo van Gogh is shot dead in Amsterdam by Mohammed Bouyeri, a Moroccan by descent, who is enraged by van Gogh's cinematic treatment of Islam. Across the country, race relations become tense.

2007 Amsterdam city council moves to restrict and reduce its Red Light District. The first of several similar initiatives.

2008 Work is halted on the underground Noord-Zuidlijn metro line. Ballooning costs, tunnels filled with water and the foundations of several old houses undermined. The line is finally completed in 2018.

2008–present Ongoing disputes concerning the city's coffeeshops, whose future looks precarious, with many Dutch dismayed by drug tourism into the Netherlands.

2013 Queen Beatrix abdicates after 33 years on the throne and is succeeded by Prince Willem-Alexander (b.1967).

2015 The number of visitors to Amsterdam soars to seventeen million. Much concern as house prices soar and local shops disappear.

2018 Femke Halsema of the Green Party becomes the first female mayor of Amsterdam.

2020 In February, the Dutch record their first case of COVID-19. Thereafter, in a pattern familiar across the rest of Europe, lock downs are imposed and then relaxed until a vaccination programme blunts the virus – or at least keeps it at bay.

2023 The city banned smoking marijuana in public areas in and around the Red Light District.

2025 Amsterdam celebrates its 750th anniversary, with celebrations across the city including the burial of a time capsule in Dam Square. The capsule will be opened in 2075.

Dutch

It's unlikely that you'll need to speak anything other than English while you're in Amsterdam. The following Dutch words and phrases may, however be useful; note that menus are nearly always multilingual.

Words and phrases

Basics and greetings

yes ja
no nee
please alstublieft
(no) thank you (nee) dank u or bedankt
hello hallo or dag
good morning goedemorgen
good afternoon goedemiddag
good evening goedenavond
goodbye tot ziens
do you speak English? spreekt u Engels?
I don't understand Ik begrijp het niet
women/men vrouwen/mannen
children kinderen

Numbers

0 nul
1 een
2 twee

3 drie
4 vier
5 vijf
6 zes
7 zeven
8 acht
9 negen
10 tien
11 elf
12 twaalf
13 dertien
14 veertien
15 vijftien
16 zestien
17 zeventien
18 achttien
19 negentien
20 twintig
21 een en twintig
22 twee en twintig
30 dertig
40 veertig
50 vijftig
60 zestig
70 zeventig
80 tachtig
90 negentig
100 honderd
101 honderd een
1000 duizend

Food and drink

Basics

boter butter
boterham/broodje sandwich/roll
brood bread
dranken drinks
eieren eggs
erwtensoep/snert pea soup with bacon or sausage
groenten vegetables
honing honey
hoofdgerechten main courses
kaas cheese
koud cold
nagerechten desserts
patates/frites chips/French fries
sla/salade salad
smeerkaas cheese spread
stokbrood French bread
suiker sugar
uitsmijter ham or cheese with eggs on bread
vis fish
vlees meat
voorgerechten starters
vruchten fruit
warm hot
zout salt

Meat and poultry

biefstuk (hollandse) steak
biefstuk (duitse) hamburger
eend duck
fricandeau roast pork
fricandel frankfurter-like sausage
gehakt minced meat
ham ham
kalfsvlees veal
kalkoen turkey
karbonade chop
kip chicken
lamsvlees lamb
lever liver
spek bacon
worst sausages

Fish

garnalen prawns
haring herring
haringsalade herring salad
kabeljauw cod
makreel mackerel
mosselen mussels
oesters oysters
paling eel
schelvis haddock
schol plaice
tong sole
zalm salmon

Vegetables

aardappelen potatoes
bloemkool cauliflower
bonen beans
champignons mushrooms
erwten peas
hutspot mashed potatoes and carrots
knoflook garlic

komkommer cucumber
prei leek
rijst rice
sla salad, lettuce
uien onions
wortelen carrots
zuurkool sauerkraut

Cooking terms

belegd filled or topped
doorbakken well-done
gebakken fried/baked
gebraden roasted
gegrild grilled
gekookt boiled
gerookt smoked
gestoofd stewed
half doorbakken medium-done
rood rare

Sweets and desserts

appelgebak apple tart or cake
gebak pastry
IJs ice cream
koekjes biscuits
oliebollen doughnuts
pannekoeken pancakes
poffertjes small pancakes, fritters
(slag)room (whipped) cream
speculaas spice and honey-flavoured biscuit
stroopwafels waffles
taai-taai Dutch honey cake
vla custard

Drinks

bessenjenever blackcurrant gin
droog dry
frisdranken soft drinks
jenever Dutch gin
karnemelk buttermilk
koffie coffee
koffie verkeerd coffee with warm milk
kopstoot beer with a jenever chaser
melk milk
pils Dutch beer
proost! cheers!
sinaasappelsap orange juice
thee tea
vruchtensap fruit juice
warme chocolademelk hot chocolate
wijn (wit/rood/rosé) wine (white/red/rosé)
vieux Dutch brandy
zoet sweet

Publishing Information

Sixth edition 2026

MIX
Paper from responsible sources
FSC® C014138
FSC www.fsc.org

Distribution

UK, Ireland and Europe
Apa Publications (UK) Ltd; mail@roughguides.com
United States and Canada
Two Rivers; ips@ingramcontent.com
Australia and New Zealand
Woodslane; info@woodslane.com.au
Worldwide
Apa Publications (UK) Ltd; mail@roughguides.com

Special Sales, Content Licensing and CoPublishing

Rough Guides can be purchased in bulk quantities at discounted prices. We can create special editions, personalized jackets and corporate imprints tailored to your needs. mail@roughguides.com.
roughguides.com

EU Representative

LOGOS EUROPE, 9 rue Nicolas Poussin, 17000, LA ROCHELLE, France; Contact@logoseurope.eu; +33 (0) 667937378
Printed by Finidr in Czech Republic.
ISBN: 9781835294437
This book was produced using **Typefi** automated publishing software.
A catalogue record for this book is available from the British Library.

Rough Guide Credits

Editor: Beth Williams
Cartography: Katie Bennett
Picture manager: Tom Smyth
Layout: Danielle Titmas
Original design: Richard Czapnik
Publishing technology manager: Rebeka Davies
Production operations manager: Katie Bennett
Head of Publishing: Sarah Clark

About the author

Beth Williams is a travel writer and editor for Rough Guides. She has lived in the USA and Germany before returning home to East London. Her adventures have taken her to Vietnam, Japan, the USA and much of continental Europe. She enjoys seeking out new dishes she hasn't tried before and firmly believes there's no better way to learn about a country than by visiting its local food markets.

Help us update

We've gone to a lot of effort to ensure that this edition of the **Pocket Rough Guide Amsterdam** is accurate and up-to-date. However, things change – places get "discovered", restaurants and rooms raise prices or lower standards, and businesses cease trading. If you feel we've got it wrong or left something out, we'd like to know, and if you can direct us to the web address, so much the better.

Please send your comments with the subject line "**Pocket Rough Guide Amsterdam Update**" to mail@roughguides.com. We'll send a copy of the next edition (or any other Rough Guide if you prefer) for the very best emails.

Photo Credits

(Key: T-top; C-centre; B-bottom; L-left; R-right)
Alamy 14B, 15B, 16T, 17B, 47, 51, 59, 70, 72, 74, 79, 83, 84, 99, 107
Anne Frank Huis 46
Conservatorium Hotel 95
De Belhamel 57
De Hortus 77
Dominic Milton Trott 103
James Stokes/The Dylan 112/113
Jan Bartelsman/Bubbles & Wines 40
Jeroen Oerlemans/Amsterdam Museum 14T
John Lewis Marshall/Stedelijk Museum 91
Joris Bruring/Bruring Media B.V/ Paradiso 16B
Leading Hotels of the World 104
Mark Thomas/Rough Guides 6, 17T, 19T, 20T, 20C, 21T, 34, 37, 38, 50, 67, 73, 87
Natascha Sturny/Rough Guide 28, 31, 33, 53, 61, 85, 93
Public domain 69, 76
Rijksmuseum 11B, 89
Roger Norum/Rough Guides 11T, 19B, 64, 86
Shutterstock 1, 2T, 2BL, 2C, 2BR, 4, 5, 10, 12T, 12B, 13T, 13B, 15T, 18T, 18C, 18B, 19C, 20B, 21C, 21B, 22/23, 24, 48, 55, 63, 66, 80, 92, 97, 102, 105, 109, 110, 120/121
Tim Draper/Rough Guides 42

Cover: Pythonbrug **Shutterstock**

Index

A

B

C

T

Z

BENEFITS OF PLANNING AND BOOKING AT ROUGHGUIDES.COM/TRIPS

PLAN YOUR ADVENTURE WITH LOCAL EXPERTS

Rough Guides' English-speaking local experts are hand-picked, based on their experience in the travel industry and their impeccable standards of customer service.

SAVE TIME AND GET ACCESS TO LOCAL KNOWLEDGE

When a local expert plans your trip, you save time and money when you book, even during high season. You won't be charged for using a credit card either.

MAKE TRAVEL A BREEZE: BOOK WITH PEACE OF MIND

Enjoy stress-free travel when you use Rough Guides' secure online booking platform. All bookings come with a money-back guarantee.

WHAT DO OTHER TRAVELLERS THINK ABOUT ROUGH GUIDES TRIPS?

Trip to Spain

This Spain tour company did a fantastic job to make our dream trip perfect. We gave them our travel budget, told them where we would like to go, and they did all of the planning. Our drivers and tour guides were always on time and very knowledgable. The hotel accommodations were better than we would have found on our own. Only one time did we end up in a location that we had not intended to be in. We called the 24 hour phone number, and they immediately fixed the situation.

Don A, USA

Trip to Morocco

Our trip was fantastic! Transportation, accommodations, guides – all were well chosen! The hotels were well situated, well appointed and had helpful, friendly staff. All of the guides we had were very knowledgeable, patient, and flexible with our varied interests in the different sites. We particularly enjoyed the side trip to Tangier! Well done! The itinerary you arranged for us allowed maximum coverage of the country with time in each city for seeing the important places.

Sharon, USA